From th[e]

Welcome to our extra-special new astrological forecast which takes you up to the end of the century on Dec[ember 31st 1999. When we first started] our year-ahead guides all the astrological calculations had to be made using tables and a calculator. Today, by the miracle of computers, we have been able to build our knowledge and hard work into a program which calculates the precise astrological aspect for every day in a flash.

When Shakespeare wrote 'The fault, dear Brutus, is not in our stars, but in ourselves', he spoke for every astrologer. In our day-to-day forecasts we cannot hope to be 100% accurate every time, because this would remove the most important influence in your life, which is you! What we can hope to do is to give you a sense of the astrological backdrop to the day, week or month in question, and so prompt you to think a little harder about what is going in your own life, and thus help improve your chances of acting effectively to deal with events and situations.

During the course of a year, there may be one or two readings that are similar in nature. This is not an error, it is simply that the Moon or a planet has repeated a particular pattern. In addition, a planetary pattern that applies to your sign may apply to someone else's sign at some other point during the year. One planetary 'return' that you already know well is the Solar return that occurs every year on your birthday.

If you've read our guides before, you'll know that we're never less than positive and that our advice is unpretentious, down to earth, and rooted in daily experience. If this is the first time you've met us, please regard us not as in any way astrological gurus, but as good friends who wish you nothing but health, prosperity and contentment. Happy 1998-9!

Sasha Fenton is a world-renowned astrologer, palmist and Tarot card reader, with over 80 books published on Astrology, Palmistry, Tarot and other forms of divination. Now living in London, Sasha is a regular broadcaster on radio and television, as well as making frequent contributions to newspapers and magazines around the world, including South Africa and Australia. She is a former President and Secretary of the British Astrological and Psychic Society (BAPS) and Secretary of the Advisory Panel on Astrological Education.

Jonathan Dee is an astrologer, artist and historian based in Wales, and a direct descendant of the great Elizabethan alchemist and wizard Dr John Dee, court astrologer to Queen Elizabeth I. He has written a number of books, including the recently completed *The Chronicles of Ancient Egypt,* and for the last five years has co-written an annual astrological forecast series with Sasha Fenton. A regular broadcaster on television and radio, he has also hosted the Starline show for KQED Talk Radio, New Mexico.

YOUR DAY-BY-DAY FORECAST
SEPTEMBER 1998 – DECEMBER 1999

PISCES

SASHA FENTON • JONATHAN DEE

HALDANE • MASON

Zambezi

DEDICATION
For the memory of Gary Bailey, a new star in heaven.

ACKNOWLEDGEMENTS
With many thanks to our computer wizard, Sean Lovatt.

This edition published 1998
by Haldane Mason Ltd
59 Chepstow Road
London W2 5BP

Copyright © Sasha Fenton and Jonathan Dee 1998

All rights reserved. No part of this publication may be reproduced, stored in a retrieval system, or transmitted, in any form or by any means, electronic, mechanical, photocopying, recording or otherwise, without the prior permission of the publishers.

Sasha Fenton and Jonathan Dee assert the moral right to be identified as the authors of this work.

ISBN 1-902463-10-2

Designed and produced by Haldane Mason Ltd
Cover illustration by Lo Cole
Edited by Jan Budkowski

Printed in Singapore by Craft Print Pte Ltd

CONTENTS

AN ASTROLOGICAL OVERVIEW OF THE 20TH CENTURY	6
THE ESSENTIAL PISCES	16
YOUR SUN SIGN	20
ALL THE OTHER SUN SIGNS	21
YOU AND YOURS	29
YOUR RISING SIGN	36
PISCES IN LOVE	41
YOUR PROSPECTS FOR 1999	43
PISCES IN THE FINAL QUARTER OF 1998	46
PISCES IN 1999	69

An Astrological Overview of the 20th Century

Next year the shops will be full of astrology books for the new century and also for the new millennium. In this book, the last of the old century, we take a brief look back to see where the slow-moving outer planets were in each decade and what it meant. Obviously this will be no more than a very brief glance backwards but next year you will be able to see the picture in much more depth when we bring out our own book for the new millennium.

1900 - 1909
The century began with Pluto in Gemini and it was still in Gemini by the end of the decade. Neptune started out in Gemini but moved into cancer in 1901 and ended the decade still in Cancer. Uranus started the century in Sagittarius, moving to Capricorn in 1904 and ending the decade still in Capricorn. Saturn began the century in Sagittarius, moving to Capricorn in January 1900 and then through Aquarius, Pisces and Aries, ending the decade in Aries.

The stars and the decade
In general terms, the planet of upheaval in the dynastic sign of Sagittarius with Saturn also in that sign and Pluto opposing it, all at the very start of the century put the spotlight on dynasties, royalty and empires. As Saturn left for the 'establishment' sign of Capricorn these just about held together but as the decade ended, the power and control that these ancient dynasties had were loosening their grip on the developed world of the time. Queen Victoria died in 1901 and her son, Edward VII was dying by the end of the decade, so in Britain, the Victorian age of certainty was already coming to an end. The Boer War was only just won by Britain in 1902 which brought a shock to this successful colonial country.

Pluto in Gemini brought a transformation in methods of communications. It was as Saturn entered the innovative sign of Aquarius that these took concrete and useful form. Thus it was during this decade that the motor car, telephone, typewriter, gramophone and colour photography came into existence. Air travel began in 1900 with the first Zeppelin airship flight, the first powered aeroplane flight by the Wright brothers in 1904 and Louis Blériot's flight across the English Channel in 1909. Edison demonstrated the Kinetophone, the first machine capable of showing talking moving pictures in

PISCES

1910. Even the nature of war changed as technologically modern Japan managed to fight off the might of the Russian empire in the war of 1904 - 1905.

The Treaty of Versailles, followed by further treaties of Aix and Trianon served to crush the German nation and therefore sow the seeds of the next war.

1910 - 1919
Pluto opened the decade in Gemini, moving to Cancer in 1913. Neptune travelled from Cancer to Leo in September 1914 while Uranus moved out of Capricorn, through Aquarius to end the decade in Pisces. Saturn moved from Aries to Taurus, then to Gemini, back into Taurus, then into Gemini again entering Cancer in 1914, then on through Leo and ending the decade in Virgo.

The stars and the decade
Now we see the start of a pattern. Sagittarius may be associated with dynasties but it is the home-loving and patriotic signs of Cancer and Leo that actually seem to be associated with major wars. The desire either to expand a country's domestic horizons or to protect them from the expansion of others is ruled by the maternal sign of Cancer, followed by the paternal one of Leo. Home, family, tradition, safety all seem to be fought over when major planets move through these signs. When future generations learn about the major wars of the 20th century they will probably be lumped together in their minds - despite the 20-year gap between them - just as we lump the Napoleonic wars together, forgetting that there was a nine-year gap between them, and of course, this long stay of Pluto in Cancer covered the whole of this period.

It is interesting to note that Pluto moved into Cancer in July 1913 and Neptune entered Leo on the 23rd of September 1914, just three of weeks after the outbreak of the First World War. Saturn moved into Cancer in April 1914. Pluto is associated with transformation, Neptune with dissolution and Saturn with loss, sadness and sickness. Many people suffered and so many families and dynasties were unexpectedly dissolved at that time, among these, the Romanov Czar and his family and the kings of Portugal, Hungary, Italy and Germany and the Manchu dynasty of China. America (born on the 4th of July, 1776 and therefore a Cancerian country) was thrust into prominence as a major economic and social power after this war. Russia experienced the Bolshevik revolution during it. As Saturn moved into Virgo (the sign that is associated with health) at the end of this decade, a world-wide plague of influenza killed 20 million people, far more than had died during the course of the war itself.

PISCES

1920 - 1929

The roaring 20s began and ended with Pluto in Cancer. Neptune moved from Leo to Virgo at the end of this decade and Uranus moved from Pisces to Aries in 1927. Saturn travelled from Virgo, through Libra, Scorpio, Sagittarius and then backwards and forwards between Sagittarius and Capricorn, ending up in Capricorn at the end of 1929.

The stars and the decade

Pluto's long transformative reign in Cancer made life hard for men during this time. Cancer is the most female of all the signs, being associated with nurturing and motherhood. Many men were sick in mind and body as a result of the war and women began to take proper jobs for the first time. Family planning and better living conditions brought improvements in life for ordinary people and in the developed world there was a major boom in house building as well as in improved road and rail commuter systems. The time of lords and ladies was passing and ordinary people were demanding better conditions. Strikes and unrest were common, especially in Germany. As the decade ended, the situation both domestically and in the foreign policies of the developed countries began to look up. Even the underdeveloped countries began to modernize a little. Shortly before the middle of this decade, all the politicians who might have prevented the rise of Hitler and the Nazi party died and then came the stock market crash of 1929. The probable astrological sequence that set this train of circumstances off was the run up to the opposition of Saturn in Capricorn to Pluto in Cancer which took place in 1931. The effects of such major planetary events are often felt while the planets are closing into a conjunction or opposition etc., rather than just at the time of their exactitude.

On a brighter note great strides were made in the worlds of art, music and film and ordinary people could enjoy more entertainment than ever before, in 1929 the first colour television was demonstrated and in 1928 Alexander Fleming announced his discovery of penicillin. At the very start of the decade prohibition passed into US Federal law, ushering in the age of organized crime and as a spin-off a great increase in drinking in that country and later on, all those wonderful gangster films. The same year, the partition of Ireland took place bringing more conflict and this time on a very long-term basis.

1930 - 1939

The 1930s should have been better than the 1920s but they were not. Pluto remained in Cancer until 1937, Neptune remained in Virgo throughout the decade, Uranus entered Taurus in 1934 and Saturn moved from Capricorn

PISCES

through Aquarius, Pisces then back and forth between Aries and Pisces, ending the decade in Taurus.

The stars and the decade
Neptune's voyage through Virgo did help in the field of advances in medicine and in public health. Pluto continued to make life hard for men and then by extension for families, while in the 'motherhood' sign of Cancer. While Saturn was in the governmental signs of Capricorn and Aquarius, democracy ceased to exist anywhere in the world. In the UK a coalition government was in power for most of the decade while in the USA, Franklin Delano Roosevelt ruled as a kind of benign emperor for almost three terms of office, temporarily dismantling much of that country's democratic machinery while he did so. Governments in Russia, Germany, Italy, Spain and Japan moved to dictatorships or dictatorial types of government with all the resultant tyranny, while France, Britain and even the USA floundered for much of the time. China was ruled by warring factions. However, there was an upsurge of popular entertainment at this time, especially through the mediums of film, music and radio probably due to the advent of adventurous, inventive Uranus into the music and entertainment sign of Taurus in 1934.

1940 - 1949
War years once again. Pluto remained in the 'paternal' sign of Leo throughout this decade, bringing tyranny and control of the masses in all the developed countries and also much of the Third World. Neptune entered Libra in 1942, Uranus moved from Taurus to Gemini in 1941, then to Cancer in 1948. Saturn began the decade in Taurus, moved to Gemini, Cancer, Leo and finally Virgo during this decade. The 'home and country' signs of Cancer and Leo were once more thrust into the limelight in a war context. Neptune is not a particularly warlike planet and Libra is normally a peaceable sign but Libra does rule open enemies as well as peace and harmony.

The stars and the decade
To continue looking for the moment at the planet Neptune, astrologers don't take its dangerous side seriously enough. Neptune can use the sea in a particularly destructive manner when it wants to with tidal waves, disasters at sea and so on, so it is interesting to note that the war in the West was almost lost for the allies at sea due to the success of the German U-boats. Hitler gambled on a quick end to the war in the east and shut his mind to Napoleon's experience of the Russian winter. Saturn through Cancer and Leo, followed by the inventive sign of Uranus entering Cancer at the end of

the decade almost brought home, family, tradition and the world itself to an end with the explosions of the first atomic bombs.

However, towards the end of this decade, it became clear that democracy, the rights of ordinary people and a better lifestyle for everybody were a better answer than trying to find 'lebensraum' by pinching one's neighbour's land and enslaving its population. Saturn's entry into Virgo brought great advances in medicine and the plagues and diseases of the past began to diminish throughout the world. Pluto in Leo transformed the power structures of every country and brought such ideas as universal education, better housing and social security systems - at least in the developed world.

1950 - 1959

Pluto still dipped in and out of Leo until it finally left for Virgo in 1957. Neptune finally left Libra for Scorpio in 1955, Uranus sat on that dangerous and warlike cusp of Cancer and Leo, while Saturn moved swiftly through Virgo, Libra, Scorpio, Sagittarius and then into Capricorn.

The stars and the decade

The confrontations between dictators and between dictatorships and democracy continued during this time with the emphasis shifting to the conflict between communism and capitalism. The Korean war started the decade and the communist take-over in China ended it. Military alertness was reflected in the UK by the two years of national service that young men were obliged to perform throughout the decade. Rationing, shortages of food, fuel and consumer goods remained in place for half the decade, but by the end of it, the world was becoming a very different place. With American money, Germany and Japan were slowly rebuilt, communism did at least bring a measure of stability in China and the Soviet Union, although its pervasive power brought fear and peculiar witch hunts in the United States. In Europe and the USA the lives of ordinary people improved beyond belief.

Pluto in Virgo brought plenty of work for the masses and for ordinary people, poverty began to recede for the first time in history. Better homes, labour-saving devices and the vast amount of popular entertainment in the cinema, the arts, popular music and television at long last brought fun into the lives of most ordinary folk. In Britain and the Commonwealth, in June 1953, the coronation of the new Queen ushered in a far more optimistic age while her Empire dissolved around her.

PISCES

1960 - 1969

This is the decade that today's middle-aged folk look back on with fond memories, yet it was not always as safe as we like to think. Pluto remained in Virgo throughout the decade bringing work and better health to many people. Neptune remained in Scorpio throughout this time, while Uranus traversed back and forth between Leo and Virgo, then from Virgo to Libra, ending the decade in Libra. Saturn hovered around the cusp of Taurus and Gemini until the middle of the decade and then on through Gemini and Cancer, spending time around the Cancer/Leo cusp and then on through Leo to rest once again on the Leo/Virgo cusp.

The stars and the decade

The Cancer/Leo threats of atomic war were very real in the early 1960s, with the Cuban missile crisis bringing America and the Soviet Union to the point of war. The Berlin wall went up. President Kennedy's assassination in November 1963 shocked the world and the atmosphere of secrets, spies and mistrust abounded in Europe, the USA and in the Soviet Union. One of the better manifestations of this time of cold war, CIA dirty tricks and spies was the plethora of wonderful spy films and television programmes of the early 60s. Another was the sheer fun of the Profumo affair!

The late 1960s brought the start of a very different atmosphere. The Vietnam War began to be challenged by the teenagers whose job it was to die in it and the might of America was severely challenged by these tiny Vietcong soldiers in black pyjamas and sandals. The wave of materialism of the 1950s was less attractive to the flower-power generation of the late 60s. The revolutionary planet Uranus in balanced Libra brought the protest movement into being and an eventual end to racial segregation in the USA. Equality between the sexes was beginning to be considered. The troubles of Northern Ireland began at the end of this decade.

In 1969, Neil Armstrong stepped out onto the surface of the Moon, thereby marking the start of a very different age, the New Age, the Age of Aquarius.

1970 - 1979

Pluto began the decade around the Virgo/Libra cusp, settling in Libra in 1972 and remaining there for the rest of the decade. Neptune started the decade by moving back and forth between Scorpio and Sagittarius and residing in Sagittarius for the rest of the decade. Uranus hovered between Libra and Scorpio until 1975 and then travelled through Scorpio until the end of the decade while Saturn moved from Taurus to Gemini, then hung around the Cancer/Leo cusp and finally moved into Virgo.

PISCES

The stars and the decade

The planets in or around that dangerous Cancer/Leo cusp and the continuing Libran emphasis brought more danger from total war as America struggled with Vietnam and the cold war. However, the influence of Virgo brought work, an easier life and more hope than ever to ordinary people in the First World. Uranus in Libra brought different kinds of love partnerships into public eye as fewer people bothered to marry. Divorce became easier and homosexuality became legal. With Uranus opening the doors to secretive Scorpio, spies such as Burgess, Maclean, Philby, Lonsdale and Penkowski began to come in from the cold. President Nixon was nicely caught out at Watergate, ushering in a time of more openness in governments everywhere.

If you are reading this book, you may be doing so because you are keen to know about yourself and your sign, but you are likely to be quite interested in astrology and perhaps in other esoteric techniques. You can thank the atmosphere of the 1970s for the openness and the lack of fear and superstition which these subjects now enjoy. The first festival of Mind, Body and Spirit took place in 1976 and the British Astrological and Psychic Society was launched in the same year, both of these events being part of the increasing interest in personal awareness and alternative lifestyles.

Neptune in Scorpio brought fuel crises and Saturn through Cancer and Leo brought much of the repression of women to an end, with some emancipation from tax and social anomalies. Tea bags and instant coffee allowed men for the first time to cope with the terrible hardship of making a cuppa!

1980 - 1989

Late in 1983, Pluto popped into the sign of Scorpio, popped out again and re-entered it in 1984. Astrologers of the 60s and 70s feared this planetary situation in case it brought the ultimate Plutonic destruction with it. Instead of this, the Soviet Union and South Africa freed themselves from tyranny and the Berlin Wall came down. The main legacy of Pluto in Scorpio is the Scorpionic association of danger through sex, hence the rise of AIDS. Neptune began the decade in Sagittarius then it travelled back and forth over the Sagittarius/Capricorn cusp, ending the decade in Capricorn. Uranus moved from Scorpio, back and forth over the Scorpio/Sagittarius cusp, then through Sagittarius, ending the decade in Capricorn. Saturn began the decade in Virgo, then hovered around the Virgo/Libra cusp, through Libra, Scorpio and Sagittarius, resting along the Sagittarius/Capricorn cusp, ending the decade in Capricorn.

PISCES

The stars and the decade
The movement of planets through the dynastic sign of Sagittarius brought doubt and uncertainty to Britain's royal family, while the planets in authoritative Capricorn brought strong government to the UK in the form of Margaret Thatcher. Ordinary people began to seriously question the *status quo* and to attempt to change it. Even in the hidden empire of China, modernization and change began to creep in. Britain went to war again by sending the gunboats to the Falkland Islands to fight off a truly old-fashioned takeover bid by the daft Argentinean dictator, General Galtieri.

Saturn is an earth planet, Neptune rules the sea, while Uranus is associated with the air. None of these planets was in their own element and this may have had something to do with the increasing number of natural and man-made disasters that disrupted the surface of the earth during this decade. The first space shuttle flight took place in 1981 and the remainder of the decade reflected many people's interest in extra-terrestrial life in the form of films and television programmes. ET went home. Black rap music and the casual use of drugs became a normal part of the youth scene. Maybe the movement of escapist Neptune through the 'outer space' sign of Sagittarius had something to do with this.

1990 - 1999
Pluto began the decade in Scorpio, moving in and out of Sagittarius until 1995 remaining there for the rest of the decade. Neptune began the decade in Capricorn, travelling back and forth over the cusp of Aquarius, ending the decade in Aquarius, Uranus moved in and out of Aquarius, remaining there from 1996 onwards. Saturn travelled from Capricorn, through Aquarius, Pisces (and back again), then on through Pisces, Aries, in and out of Taurus, finally ending the decade in Taurus.

The stars and the decade
The Aquarian emphasis has brought advances in science and technology and a time when computers are common even in the depths of darkest Africa. The logic and fairness of Aquarius does seem to have affected many of the peoples of the earth. Pluto in the open sign of Sagittarius brought much governmental secrecy to an end, it will also transform the traditional dynasties of many countries before it leaves them for good. The aftermath of the dreadful and tragic death of Princess Diana in 1997 put a rocket under the creaking 19th-century habits of British royalty.

The final decade began with yet another war – this time the Gulf War – which sent a serious signal to all those who fancy trying their hand at

PISCES

international bullying or the 19th-century tactics of pinching your neighbour's land and resources. Uranus's last fling in Capricorn tore up the earth with volcanoes and earthquakes, and its stay in Aquarius seems to be keeping this pattern going. Saturn in Pisces, opposite the 'health' sign of Virgo is happily bringing new killer viruses into being and encouraging old ones to build up resistance to antibiotics. The bubonic plague is alive and well in tropical countries along with plenty of other plagues that either are, or are becoming resistant to modern medicines. Oddly enough the planetary line-up in 1997 was similar to that of the time of the great plague of London in 1665!

Films, the arts, architecture all showed signs of beginning an exciting period of revolution in 1998. Life became more electronic and computer-based for the younger generation while in the old world, the vast army of the elderly began to struggle with a far less certain world of old-age poverty and strange and frightening innovations. Keeping up to date and learning to adapt is the only way to survive now, even for the old folks.

It is interesting to note that the first event of importance to shock Europe in this century was the morganatic marriage of Franz Ferdinand, the heir to the massively powerful Austro-Hungarian throne. This took place in the summer of 1900. The unpopularity of this controlling and repressive empire fell on its head in Sarajevo on the 28th of July 1914. This mighty empire is now almost forgotten, but its death throes are still being played out in and around Sarajevo today - which only goes to show how long it can take for anything to be settled.

Technically the twentieth century only ends at the beginning of the year 2001 but most of us will be celebrating the end of the century and the end of the millennium and the end of the last day of 1999 - that is if we are all here of course! A famous prediction of global disaster comes from the writings of the French writer, doctor and astrologer Nostradamus (1503–66):

- The year 1999, seventh month,
- From the sky will come a great King of Terror:
- To bring back to life the great King of the Mongols,
- Before and after Mars reigns.
  (Quatrain X:72 from the *Centuries*)

Jonathan has worked out that with the adjustments of the calendar from the time of Nostradamus, the date of the predicted disaster will be the 11th of August 1999. As it happens there will be a total eclipse of the Sun at ten past eleven on that day at 18 degrees of Leo. We have already seen how the signs of Cancer, Leo and Libra seem to be the ones that are most clearly associated with war and this reference to 'Mars reigning' is the fact that Mars is the god of war. Therefore, the prediction suggests that an Oriental king will wage a war from the sky that brings terror to the world. Some people have suggested that this event would bring about the end of the world but that is not what the prediction actually says. A look back over the 1900s has proved this whole century to be one of terror from the skies but it would be awful to think that there would be yet another war, this time emanating from Mongolia. Terrible but not altogether impossible to imagine I guess. Well, let us hope that we are all here for us to write and for you to enjoy the next set of zodiac books for the turn of the millennium and beyond.

2000 onwards: a very brief look forward

The scientific exploration and eventual colonization of space is on the way now. Scorpio rules fossil fuels and there will be no major planets passing through this sign for quite a while so alternative fuel sources will have to be sought. Maybe it will be the entry of Uranus into the pioneering sign of Aries in January 2012 that will make a start on this. The unusual line up of the 'ancient seven' planets of Sun, Moon, Mercury, Venus, Mars and Saturn in Taurus on the 5th of May 2000 will be interesting. Taurus represents such matters as land, farming, building, cooking, flowers, the sensual beauty of music, dancing and the arts. Jonathan and Sasha will work out the astrological possibilities for the future in depth and put out ideas together for you in a future book.

PISCES

The Essential Pisces

YOUR RULING PLANET Neptune is your ruling body. The Roman god Neptune ruled the sea and all the mysterious things that are hidden beneath it. Before Neptune was discovered, your sign was said to be ruled by Jupiter.

YOUR SYMBOL Two fish tied together and swimming in different directions is the symbol for your sign. The Babylonians knew the constellation of Pisces as 'Kun', which means 'the tails'. This is very appropriate for the last sign of the zodiac. It was also known as the leash which was the link between the two fish. The symbol itself may commemorate the occasion when Venus and Cupid disguised themselves as fish in order to escape from the angry giant.

PARTS OF THE BODY The feet, but also the mind and the psychic and intuitive faculties. Also the lungs.

YOUR GOOD BITS You are imaginative, sensitive and peaceful.

YOUR BAD BITS You can be indecisive, inclined to worry over nothing and lacking in willpower.

YOUR WEAKNESSES Avoiding decisions, escapism, alcohol.

YOUR BEST DAY Thursday. The days of the week pre-date the discovery of the outer planets, therefore your day is Thursday which is Jupiter's day.

YOUR WORST DAY Wednesday.

YOUR COLOURS Sea colours, greeny-blues, turquoise, purple.

CITIES Hull, Alexandria, Seville, Christchurch, São Paulo.

COUNTRIES Portugal, New Zealand, the Sahara.

HOLIDAYS You love to be in, on or near the sea. You enjoy sea views and some of you like snorkelling and scuba diving where you can be, literally,

PISCES

in your element. You would enjoy visiting Eilat.

YOUR FAVOURITE CAR An astonishing number of Pisceans don't drive at all, while others do drive when pushed to it but prefer others to do the driving, even in your own car. If you have a vehicle at all, it is likely to be a battered old horse box, a campervan or caravan.

YOUR FAVOURITE MEAL OUT You are probably quite a good cook, therefore you can be fairly discriminating about food and service when you eat out. Many Pisceans are vegetarians or enjoy fish meals.

YOUR FAVOURITE DRINK Anything. There are even rumours that there is blood in your alcohol!

YOUR HERBS You are more attuned to spices than to herbs and clove is supposed to link with your sign. However, the herb birthwart which was supposed to ease the pains of childbirth, is also associated with Pisces.

YOUR TREE The lime.

YOUR FLOWERS Water lily, poppy. The sign of Pisces is associated with sleep and also escapism through drink and narcotics, therefore the poppy is appropriate. Apart from the modern-day horrors of drug-taking, some kinds of poppy have always been used for medicinal purposes.

YOUR ANIMALS Fish, dolphin and the mythical unicorn.

YOUR METAL Tin.

YOUR GEMS There are various gems associated with your sign, including the cool, romantic moonstone, the passionate bloodstone and the pearl.

MODE OF DRESS Pisceans simply loved the hippie era and the fancy dress of the 70s. Nowadays, you probably prefer jeans or casual clothes in gentle, romantic colours.

YOUR CAREERS Any creative or artistic profession, any branch of showbusiness and anything which helps, teaches, counsels or heals people. There are numerous Piscean Tarot-card readers, mediums, healers, psychotherapists, teachers and astrologers.

PISCES

YOUR FRIENDS You prefer people who are sympathetic, good listeners and who have a good sense of humour.

YOUR ENEMIES Cold, logical people and heartless ones who are cruel to animals or children.

YOUR FAVOURITE GIFT You may be eccentric but you do appreciate a touch of luxury. Therefore a good-quality gift that reflects your special interest would suit you. You may collect china animals or Japanese tea sets, so an addition to your collection would be nice. A visit to a psychic or a medium would please you. Also a collection of old films on video, fishing tackle, perfume, CDs, a nice pair of slippers and of course booze!

YOUR IDEAL HOME Preferably by the sea or some other source of water. You may have a flat in town and a house by the sea. Otherwise, anything unusual such as a converted church or railway station might suit you. Whatever you choose to live in, there must be a pub near by!

YOUR FAVOURITE BOOKS Poetry, song lyrics, books that show you how to make craft items, books on astrology or mystical subjects, science fiction, adventure stories and a recipe book that shows you twenty-seven different ways of preparing beans!

YOUR FAVOURITE MUSIC You really understand and appreciate music, so whether it's pop or classical it must be well performed and if on CD, the best orchestra and the best-quality recording you can find. You might enjoy ballads or ballet music or simply something that reminds you of the past. You probably like meditation music with dolphins, birds and whales singing along to the tune (or lack of it)!

YOUR GAMES AND SPORTS Oddly enough, Pisceans are quite sporty in various ways. You enjoy walking, aerobics, swimming and, above all, dancing. You love to travel and you may enjoy fishing.

YOUR PAST AND FUTURE LIVES There are many theories about past lives and even some about future ones, but we suggest that your immediate past life was ruled by the sign previous to Pisces and that your future life will be governed by the sign following Pisces. You were therefore Aquarius in your previous life and will be Aries in the next.

PISCES

If you want to know all about either of these signs, zip straight out to the shops and buy our books on them!

YOUR LUCKY NUMBER Your lucky number is 3. To find your lucky number on a raffle ticket or something similar, first add the numbers together. For example, if one of your lottery numbers is 28, add 2 + 8 to make 10; then add 1 + 0, to give the root number of 1. The number 316 on a raffle ticket works in the same way. Add 3 + 1 + 6 to make 10: then add 1 + 0, making 1. As your lucky number is anything that adds up to 3, numbers such as 21, 147 or 30 would work. A selection of lottery numbers should include at least some of the following: 3, 12, 30, 39 and 48.

PISCES

Your Sun Sign

*Your Sun Sign is determined by your date of birth.
Thus anyone born between 21st March and 20th April is Aries and so
on through the calendar. Your Rising Sign (see page 36)
is determined by the day and time of your birth.*

PISCES

RULED BY JUPITER AND NEPTUNE
20th February to 20th March

Yours is a feminine, water sign whose symbol is two fishes, tied together and swimming in opposite directions. This gives you a strange mixture of qualities, all wrapped up in one personality. On some occasions you can be extremely practical and businesslike, while at other times you are dreamy, impractical and helpless. However, when that happens, you have the happy knack of drawing efficient, resourceful, well-organized people to you to help out when the going gets tough.

Many of you work in the caring professions as teachers, nurses or in animal welfare, while others work in artistic or creative fields or in some form of restoration or preservation. You can be quite astute in business because your strong intuition tells you who to trust or how far to go with a particular scheme. A few of you find the right avenue for your particular talents very early on, but most of you will try out a number of different careers during your lifetime. Problems come when you lose faith in the people you work for or when you get bored with what you are doing. You could get ill if your job became unpleasant or too pressurized, and you get very disheartened if you feel undervalued.

There is a strangely mystical side to you which draws you to religious, spiritual or New Age ideas, and many of you work as spiritual healers, mediums and Tarot readers. You are drawn to natural or alternative health therapies and you may eventually spend time working in this kind of field. One natural outlet for your talents is reflexology, because this involves treating the feet and your ruling planet, Neptune, rules the feet. Another is aromatherapy, because this deals with oils and perfumes and these too are ruled by Neptune.

You can have mixed fortunes in relationships and you must guard against drawing domineering partners to you. You must also beware of 'co-dependency' relationships. This is an American psychology buzzword for the kind of people who link up with alcoholics, drug addicts, violent partners or other unhappy souls. You should be aware of your desire to 'rescue' others or to be drawn into joining them in their addictive behaviour. Fortunately, you have an inner strength which comes to your aid. You also have a bossy streak which prevents others from walking all over you for any length of time. Some of you demand a lot of attention from a partner while others are happy to live in undemanding harmony. There is no way of categorizing you, because every Piscean is different.

You love children and will probably have a larger than average family. You make a wonderful parent and you have plenty of patience for a sensitive child. However, you expect your children to do well in life and you can become extremely disappointed with them if they don't. Many of you find animals easier to deal with than people and you may spend the later part of your life happily living with a house full of pets, or maybe on a farm. Many of you work in the caring professions such as teaching, nursing, caring for the elderly, the handicapped or deprived children. Your heart is soft but you also have a strong sense of self-preservation. One of the things you try to preserve is your money. You can be generous in big ways but surprisingly mean in small ones and, although you don't appear materialistic, you are unlikely to be broke or in debt for long.

All the Other Sun Signs

ARIES
21st March to 20th April

Ariens can get anything they want off the ground, but they may land back down again with a bump. Quick to think and to act, Ariens are often intelligent and have little patience with fools. This includes anyone who is slower than themselves.

They are not the tidiest of people and they are impatient with details, except when engaged upon their special subject; then Ariens can fiddle around for hours. They are willing to make huge financial sacrifices for their families and they can put up with relatives living with them as long as this leaves them free to do their own thing. Aries women are decisive and competitive at work but many are disinterested in homemaking. They might

PISCES

consider giving up a relationship if it interfered with their ambitions. Highly sexed and experimental, they are faithful while in love but, if love begins to fade, they start to look around. Ariens may tell themselves that they are only looking for amusement, but they may end up in a fulfilling relationship with someone else's partner. This kind of situation offers the continuity and emotional support which they need with no danger of boredom or entrapment.

Their faults are those of impatience and impetuosity, coupled with a hot temper. They can pick a furious row with a supposed adversary, tear him or her to pieces then walk away from the situation five minutes later, forgetting all about it. Unfortunately, the poor victim can't always shake off the effects of the row in quite the same way. However, Arien cheerfulness, spontaneous generosity and kindness make them the greatest friends to have.

TAURUS
21st April to 21st May

These people are practical and persevering. Taureans are solid and reliable, regular in habits, sometimes a bit wet behind the ears and stubborn as mules. Their love of money and the comfort it can bring may make them very materialistic in outlook. They are most suited to a practical career which brings with it few surprises and plenty of money. However, they have a strong artistic streak which can be expressed in work, hobbies and interests.

Some Taureans are quick and clever, highly amusing and quite outrageous in appearance, but underneath this crazy exterior is a background of true talent and very hard work. This type may be a touch arrogant. Other Taureans hate to be rushed or hassled, preferring to work quietly and thoroughly at their own pace. They take relationships very seriously and make safe and reliable partners. They may keep their worries to themselves but they are not usually liars or sexually untrustworthy.

Being so very sensual as well as patient, these people make excellent lovers. Their biggest downfall comes later in life when they have a tendency to plonk themselves down in front of the television night after night, tuning out the rest of the world. Another problem with some Taureans is their 'pet hate', which they'll harp on about at any given opportunity. Their virtues are common sense, loyalty, responsibility and a pleasant, non-hostile approach to others. Taureans are much brighter than anyone gives them credit, and it is hard to beat them in an argument because they usually know what they are talking about. If a Taurean is on your side, they make wonderful friends and comfortable and capable colleagues.

PISCES

GEMINI
22nd May to 21st June

Geminis are often accused of being short on intellect and unable to stick to anyone or anything for long. In a nutshell, great fun at a party but totally unreliable. This is unfair: nobody works harder, is more reliable or capable than Geminis when they put their mind to a task, especially if there is a chance of making large sums of money! Unfortunately, they have a low boredom threshold and they can drift away from something or someone when it no longer interests them. They like to be busy, with plenty of variety in their lives and the opportunity to communicate with others. Their forte lies in the communications industry where they shamelessly pinch ideas and improve on them. Many Geminis are highly ambitious people who won't allow anything or anyone to stand in their way.

They are surprisingly constant in relationships, often marrying for life but, if it doesn't work out, they will walk out and put the experience behind them. Geminis need relationships and if one fails, they will soon start looking for the next. Faithfulness is another story, however, because the famous Gemini curiosity can lead to any number of adventures. Geminis educate their children well while neglecting to see whether they have a clean shirt. The house is full of books, videos, televisions, CDs, newspapers and magazines and there is a phone in every room as well as in the car, the loo and the Gemini lady's handbag.

CANCER
22nd June to 23rd July

Cancerians look for security on the one hand and adventure and novelty on the other. They are popular because they really listen to what others are saying. Their own voices are attractive too. They are naturals for sales work and in any kind of advisory capacity. Where their own problems are concerned, they can disappear inside themselves and brood, which makes it hard for others to understand them. Cancerians spend a good deal of time worrying about their families and, even more so, about money. They appear soft but are very hard to influence.

Many Cancerians are small traders and many more work in teaching or the caring professions. They have a feel for history, perhaps collecting historical mementoes, and their memories are excellent. They need to have a home but they love to travel away from it, being happy in the knowledge that it is there waiting for them to come back to. There are a few Cancerians who seem to drift through life and expect other members of their family to keep them.

Romantically, they prefer to be settled and they fear being alone. A marriage would need to be really bad before they consider leaving, and if they do, they soon look for a new partner. These people can be scoundrels in business because they hate parting with money once they have their hands on it. However, their charm and intelligence usually manage to get them out of trouble.

LEO
24th July to 23rd August

Leos can be marvellous company or a complete pain in the neck. Under normal circumstances, they are warm-hearted, generous, sociable and popular but they can be very moody and irritable when under pressure or under the weather. Leos put their heart and soul into whatever they are doing and they can work like demons for a while. However, they cannot keep up the pace for long and they need to get away, zonk out on the sofa and take frequent holidays. These people always appear confident and they look like true winners, but their confidence can suddenly evaporate, leaving them unsure and unhappy with their efforts. They are extremely sensitive to hurt and they cannot take ridicule or even very much teasing.

Leos are proud. They have very high standards in all that they do and most have great integrity and honesty, but there are some who are complete and utter crooks. These people can stand on their dignity and be very snobbish. Their arrogance can become insufferable and they can take their powers of leadership into the realms of bossiness. They are convinced that they should be in charge and they can be very obstinate. Some Leos love the status and lifestyle which proclaims their successes. Many work in glamour professions such as the airline and entertainment industries. Others spend their day communing with computers and other high-tech gadgetry. In loving relationships, they are loyal but only while the magic lasts. If boredom sets in, they often start looking around for fresh fields. They are the most generous and loving of people and they need to play affectionately. Leos are kind, charming and they live life to the full.

VIRGO
24th August to 23rd September

Virgos are highly intelligent, interested in everything and everyone and happy to be busy with many jobs and hobbies. Many have some kind of specialized knowledge and most are good with their hands, but their nit-picking ways can infuriate colleagues. They find it hard to discuss their innermost feelings and this can make them hard to understand. In many ways, they are happier doing something practical than dealing with relationships. Virgos can also overdo the self-sacrificial bit and make themselves martyrs to other people's impractical lifestyles. They are willing to fit in with whatever is going on and can adjust to most things, but they mustn't neglect their own needs.

Although excellent communicators and wonderfully witty conversationalists, Virgos prefer to express their deepest feelings by actions rather than words. Most avoid touching all but very close friends and family members and many find lovey-dovey behaviour embarrassing. They can be very highly sexed and may use this as a way of expressing love. Virgos are criticized a good deal as children and are often made to feel unwelcome in their childhood homes. In turn, they become very critical of others and they can use this in order to wound.

Many Virgos overcome inhibitions by taking up acting, music, cookery or sports. Acting is particularly common to this sign because it allows them to put aside their fears and take on the mantle of someone quite different. They are shy and slow to make friends but when they do accept someone, they are the loyalest, gentlest and kindest of companions. They are great company and have a wonderful sense of humour.

LIBRA
24th September to 23rd October

Librans have a deceptive appearance, looking soft but being tough and quite selfish underneath. Astrological tradition tells us that this sign is dedicated to marriage, but a high proportion of them prefer to remain single, particularly when a difficult relationship comes to an end. These people are great to tell secrets to because they never listen to anything properly and promptly forget whatever is said. The confusion between their desire to co-operate with others and the need for self-expression is even more evident when at work. The best job is one where they are a part of an organization but able to take responsibility and make their own decisions.

While some Librans are shy and lacking in confidence, others are strong and determined with definite leadership qualities. All need to find a job that entails dealing with others and which does not wear out their delicate nerves. All Librans are charming, sophisticated and diplomatic, but can be confusing for others. All have a strong sense of justice and fair play but most haven't the strength to take on a determinedly lame duck. They project an image which is attractive, chosen to represent their sense of status and

PISCES

refinement. Being inclined to experiment sexually, they are not the most faithful of partners and even goody-goody Librans are terrible flirts.

SCORPIO
24th October to 22nd November

Reliable, resourceful and enduring, Scorpios seem to be the strong men and women of the zodiac. But are they really? They can be nasty at times, dishing out what they see as the truth, no matter how unwelcome. Their own feelings are sensitive and they are easily hurt, but they won't show any hurt or weakness in themselves to others. When they are very low or unhappy, this turns inwards, attacking their immune systems and making them ill. However, they have great resilience and they bounce back time and again from the most awful ailments.

Nobody needs to love and be loved more than a Scorpio, but their partners must stand up to them because they will give anyone they don't respect a very hard time indeed. They are the most loyal and honest of companions, both in personal relationships and at work. One reason for this is their hatred of change or uncertainty. Scorpios enjoy being the power behind the throne with someone else occupying the hot seat. This way, they can quietly manipulate everyone, set one against another and get exactly what they want from the situation.

Scorpios' voices are their best feature, often low, well-modulated and cultured and these wonderful voices are used to the full in pleasant persuasion. These people are neither as highly sexed nor as difficult as most astrology books make out, but they do have their passions (even if these are not always for sex itself) and they like to be thought of as sexy. They love to shock and to appear slightly dangerous, but they also make kind-hearted and loyal friends, superb hosts and gentle people who are often very fond of animals. Great people when they are not being cruel, stingy or devious!

SAGITTARIUS
23rd November to 21st December

Sagittarians are great company because they are interested in everything and everyone. Broad-minded and lacking in prejudice, they are fascinated by even the strangest of people. With their optimism and humour, they are often the life and soul of the party, while they are in a good mood. They can become quite down-hearted, crabby and awkward on occasion, but not usually for long. They can be hurtful to others because they cannot resist speaking what they see as the truth, even if it causes embarrassment. However, their tactlessness is usually innocent and they have no desire to hurt.

Sagittarians need an unconventional lifestyle, preferably one which allows them to travel. They cannot be cooped up in a cramped environment and they need to meet new people and to explore a variety of ideas during their day's work. Money is not their god and they will work for a pittance if they feel inspired by the task. Their values are spiritual rather than material. Many are attracted to the spiritual side of life and may be interested in the Church, philosophy, astrology and other New Age subjects. Higher education and legal matters attract them because these subjects expand and explore intellectual boundaries. Long-lived relationships may not appeal because they need to feel free and unfettered, but they can do well with a self-sufficient and independent partner. Despite all this intellectualism and need for freedom, Sagittarians have a deep need to be cuddled and touched and they need to be supported emotionally.

CAPRICORN
22nd December to 20th January

Capricorns are patient, realistic and responsible and they take life seriously. They need security but they may find this difficult to achieve. Many live on a treadmill of work, simply to pay the bills and feed the kids. They will never shun family responsibilities, even caring for distant relatives if this becomes necessary. However, they can play the martyr while doing so. These people hate coarseness, they are easily embarrassed and they hate to annoy anyone. Capricorns believe fervently in keeping the peace in their families. This doesn't mean that they cannot stand up for themselves, indeed they know how to get their own way and they won't be bullied. They are adept at using charm to get around prickly people.

Capricorns are ambitious, hard-working, patient and status-conscious and they will work their way steadily towards the top in any organization. If they run their own businesses, they need a partner with more pizzazz to deal with sales and marketing for them while they keep an eye on the books. Their nit-picking habits can infuriate others and some have a tendency to 'know best' and not to listen. These people work at their hobbies with the same kind of dedication that they put into everything else. They are faithful and reliable in relationships and it takes a great deal to make them stray. If a relationship breaks up, they take a long time to get over it. They may marry very early or delay it until middle age when they are less shy. As an earth sign, Capricorns are highly sexed but they need to be in a relationship where they can relax and gain confidence. Their best attribute is their genuine kindness and their wonderfully dry, witty sense of humour.

AQUARIUS
21st January to 19th February

Clever, friendly, kind and humane, Aquarians are the easiest people to make friends with but probably the hardest to really know. They are often more comfortable with acquaintances than with those who are close to them. Being dutiful, they would never let a member of their family go without their basic requirements, but they can be strangely, even deliberately, blind to their underlying needs and real feelings. They are more comfortable with causes and their idealistic ideas than with the day-to-day routine of family life. Their homes may reflect this lack of interest by being rather messy, although there are other Aquarians who are almost clinically house proud.

Their opinions are formed early in life and are firmly fixed. Being patient with people, they make good teachers and are, themselves, always willing to learn something new. But are they willing to go out and earn a living? Some are, many are not. These people can be extremely eccentric in the way they dress or the way they live. They make a point of being 'different' and they can actually feel very unsettled and uneasy if made to conform, even outwardly. Their restless, sceptical minds mean that they need an alternative kind of lifestyle which stretches them mentally.

In relationships, they are surprisingly constant and faithful and they only stray when they know in their hearts that there is no longer anything to be gained from staying put. Aquarians are often very attached to the first real commitment in their lives and they can even remarry a previously divorced partner. Their sexuality fluctuates, perhaps peaking for some years then pushed aside while something else occupies their energies, then high again. Many Aquarians are extremely highly sexed and very clever and active in bed.

PISCES

You and Yours

What is it like to bring up an Arien child? What kind of father does a Libran make? How does it feel to grow up with a Sagittarian mother? Whatever your own sign is, how do you appear to your parents and how do you behave towards your children?

THE PISCES FATHER
Piscean men fall into one of two categories. Some are kind and gentle, happy to take their children on outings and to introduce them to art, culture, music or sport. Others are disorganized and unpredictable. The kindly fathers don't always push their children. They encourage their kids to have friends and a pet or two.

THE PISCES MOTHER
Piscean mothers may be lax and absent-minded but they love their children and are usually loved in return. Many are too disorganized to run a perfect household so meals, laundry, etc. can be hit and miss, but their children prosper despite this, although many learn to reverse the mother/child roles. These mothers teach their offspring to appreciate animals and the environment.

THE PISCES CHILD
These sensitive children may find life difficult and they can get lost among stronger, more demanding brothers and sisters. They may drive their parents batty with their dreamy attitude and they can make a fuss over nothing. They need a secure and loving home with parents who shield them from harsh reality while encouraging them to develop their imaginative and psychic abilities.

THE ARIES FATHER
Arien men take the duties of fatherhood very seriously. They read to their children, take them on educational trips and expose them to art and music from an early age. They can push their children too hard or tyrannize the sensitive ones. The Aries father wants his children not only to have what he didn't have but also to be what he isn't. He respects those children who are high achievers and who can stand up to him.

PISCES

THE ARIES MOTHER

Arien women love their children dearly and will make amazing sacrifices for them, but don't expect them to give up their jobs or their outside interests for motherhood. Competitive herself, this mother wants her children to be the best and she may push them too hard. However, she is kind-hearted, affectionate and not likely to over-discipline them. She treats her offspring as adults and is well loved in return.

THE ARIES CHILD

Arien children are hard to ignore. Lively, noisy and demanding, they try to enjoy every moment of their childhood. Despite this, they lack confidence and need reassurance. Often clever but lacking in self-discipline, they need to be made to attend school each day and to do their homework. Active and competitive, these children excel in sports, dancing or learning to play a pop music instrument.

THE TAURUS FATHER

This man cares deeply for his children and wants the best for them, but doesn't expect the impossible. He may lay the law down and he can be unsympathetic to the attitudes and interests of a new generation. He may frighten young children by shouting at them. Being a responsible parent, he offers a secure family base but he may find it hard to let them go when they want to leave.

THE TAURUS MOTHER

These women make good mothers due to their highly domesticated nature. Some are real earth mothers, baking bread and making wonderful toys and games for their children. Sane and sensible but not highly imaginative, they do best with a child who has ordinary needs and they get confused by those who are 'special' in any way. Taurus mothers are very loving but they use reasonable discipline when necessary.

THE TAURUS CHILD

Taurean children can be surprisingly demanding. Their loud voices and stubborn natures can be irritating. Plump, sturdy and strong, some are shy and retiring, while others can bully weaker children. Artistic, sensual and often musical, these children can lose themselves in creative or beautiful hobbies. They need to be encouraged to share and express love and also to avoid too many sweet foods.

THE GEMINI FATHER

Gemini fathers are fairly laid back in their approach and, while they cope well with fatherhood, they can become bored with home life and try to escape from their duties. Some are so absorbed with work that they hardly see their offspring. At home, Gemini fathers will provide books, educational toys and as much computer equipment as the child can use, and they enjoy a family game of tennis.

THE GEMINI MOTHER

These mothers can be very pushy because they see education as the road to success. They encourage a child to pursue any interest and will sacrifice time and money for this. They usually have a job outside the home and may rely on other people to do some child-minding for them. Their children cannot always count on coming home to a balanced meal, but they can talk to their mothers on any subject.

THE GEMINI CHILD

These children needs a lot of reassurance because they often feel like square pegs in round holes. They either do very well at school and incur the wrath of less able children, or they fail dismally and have to make it up later in life. They learn to read early and some have excellent mechanical ability while others excel at sports. They get bored very easily and they can be extremely irritating.

THE CANCER FATHER

A true family man who will happily embrace even stepchildren as if they were his own. Letting go of the family when they grow up is another matter. Cancerian sulks, moodiness and bouts of childishness can confuse or frighten some children, while his changeable attitude to money can make them unsure of what they should ask for. This father enjoys domesticity and child-rearing and he may be happy to swap roles.

THE CANCER MOTHER

Cancerian women are excellent home makers and cheerful and reasonable mothers, as long as they have a part-time job or an interest outside the house. They instinctively know when a child is unhappy and can deal with it in a manner which is both efficient and loving. These women have a reputation for clinging but most are quite realistic when the time comes for their brood to leave the nest.

PISCES

THE CANCER CHILD
These children are shy, cautious and slow to grow up. They may achieve little at school, 'disappearing' behind louder and more demanding classmates. They can be worriers who complain about every ache and pain or suffer from imaginary fears. They may take on the mother's role in the family, dictating to their sisters and brothers at times. Gentle and loving but moody and secretive, they need a lot of love and encouragement.

THE LEO FATHER
These men can be wonderful fathers as long as they remember that children are not simply small and rather obstreperous adults. Leo fathers like to be involved with their children and encourage them to do well at school. They happily make sacrifices for their children and they truly want them to have the best, but they can be a bit too strict and they may demand too high a standard.

THE LEO MOTHER
Leo mothers are very caring and responsible but they cannot be satisfied with a life of pure domesticity, and need to combine motherhood with a job. These mothers don't fuss about minor details. They're prepared to put up with a certain amount of noise and disruption, but they can be irritable and they may demand too much of their children.

THE LEO CHILD
These children know almost from the day they are born that they are special. They are usually loved and wanted but they are also aware that a lot is expected from them. Leo children appear outgoing but they are surprisingly sensitive and easily hurt. They only seem to wake up to the need to study a day or so after they leave school, but they find a way to make a success of their lives.

THE VIRGO FATHER
These men may be embarrassed by open declarations of love and affection and find it hard to give cuddles and reassurance to small children. Yet they love their offspring dearly and will go to any lengths to see that they have the best possible education and outside activities. Virgoan men can become wrapped up in their work, forgetting to spend time relaxing and playing with their children.

THE VIRGO MOTHER
Virgoan women try hard to be good mothers because they probably had a poor childhood themselves. They love their children very much and want the best for them but they may be fussy about unnecessary details, such as dirt

on the kitchen floor or the state of the children's school books. If they can keep their tensions and longings away from their children, they can be the most kindly and loving parents.

THE VIRGO CHILD

Virgoan children are practical and capable and can do very well at school, but they are not always happy. They don't always fit in and they may have difficulty making friends. They may be shy, modest and sensitive and they can find it hard to live up to their own impossibly high standards. Virgo children don't need harsh discipline, they want approval and will usually respond perfectly well to reasoned argument.

THE LIBRA FATHER

Libran men mean well, but they may not actually perform that well. They have no great desire to be fathers but welcome their children when they come along. They may slide out of the more irksome tasks by having an absorbing job or a series of equally absorbing hobbies which keep them occupied outside the home. These men do better with older children because they can talk to them.

THE LIBRA MOTHER

Libran mothers are pleasant and easy-going but some of them are more interested in their looks, their furnishings and their friends than their children. Others are very loving and kind but a bit too soft, which results in their children disrespecting them or walking all over them in later life. These mothers enjoy talking to their children and encouraging them to succeed.

THE LIBRA CHILD

These children are charming and attractive and they have no difficulty in getting on with people. They make just enough effort to get through school and only do the household jobs they cannot dodge. They may drive their parents mad with their demands for the latest gadget or gimmick. However, their common sense, sense of humour and reasonable attitude makes harsh discipline unnecessary.

THE SCORPIO FATHER

These fathers can be really awful or absolutely wonderful, and there aren't any half-measures. Good Scorpio men provide love and security because they stick closely to their homes and families and are unlikely to do a disappearing act. Difficult ones can be loud and tyrannical. These proud men want their children to be the best.

THE SCORPIO MOTHER

These mothers are either wonderful or not really maternal at all, although they try to do their best. If they take to child-rearing, they encourage their offspring educationally and in their hobbies. These mothers have no time for whiny or miserable children but they respect outgoing, talented and courageous ones, and can cope with a handful.

THE SCORPIO CHILD

Scorpio children are competitive, self-centred and unwilling to co-operate with brothers, sisters, teachers or anyone else when in an awkward mood. They can be deeply unreadable, living in a world of their own and filled with all kinds of strange angry feelings. At other times, they can be delightfully caring companions. They love animals, sports, children's organizations and group activities.

THE SAGITTARIUS FATHER

Sagittarian fathers will give their children all the education they can stand. They happily provide books, equipment and take their offspring out to see anything interesting. They may not always be available to their offspring, but they make up for it by surprising their families with tickets for sporting events or by bringing home a pet for the children. These men are cheerful and childlike themselves.

THE SAGITTARIUS MOTHER

This mother is kind, easy-going and pleasant. She may be very ordinary with suburban standards or she may be unbelievably eccentric, forcing the family to take up strange diets and filling the house with weird and wonderful people. Some opt out of child-rearing by finding childminders while others take on other people's children and a host of animals in addition to their own.

THE SAGITTARIUS CHILD

Sagittarian children love animals and the outdoor life but they are just as interested in sitting around and watching the telly as the next child. These children have plenty of friends whom they rush out and visit at every opportunity. Happy and optimistic but highly independent, they cannot be pushed in any direction. Many leave home in late their teens in order to travel.

THE CAPRICORN FATHER

These are true family men who cope with housework and child-rearing but they are sometimes too involved in work to spend much time at home. Dutiful and caring, these men are unlikely to run off with a bimbo or to leave their family wanting. However, they can be stuffy or out of touch with the younger generation. They encourage their children to do well and to behave properly.

THE CAPRICORN MOTHER

Capricorn women make good mothers but they may be inclined to fuss. Being ambitious, they want their children to do well and they teach them to respect teachers, youth leaders and so on. These mothers usually find work outside the home in order to supplement the family income. They are very loving but they can be too keen on discipline and the careful management of pocket money.

THE CAPRICORN CHILD

Capricorn children are little adults from the day they are born. They don't need much discipline or encouragement to do well at school. Modest and well behaved, they are almost too good to be true. However, they suffer badly with their nerves and can be prone to ailments such as asthma. They need to be taught to let go, have fun and enjoy their childhood. Some are too selfish or ambitious to make friends.

THE AQUARIAN FATHER

Some Aquarian men have no great desire to be fathers but they make a reasonable job of it when they have to. They cope best when their children are reasonable and intelligent but, if they are not, they tune out and ignore them. Some Aquarians will spend hours inventing games and toys for their children while all of them value education and try to push their children.

THE AQUARIAN MOTHER

Some of these mothers are too busy putting the world to rights to see what is going on in their own family. However, they are kind, reasonable and keen on education. They may be busy outside the house but they often take their children along with them. They are not fussy homemakers, and are happy to have all the neighbourhood kids in the house. They respect a child's dignity.

THE AQUARIAN CHILD

These children may be demanding when very young but they become much more reasonable when at school. They are easily bored and need outside interests. They have many friends and may spend more time in other people's homes than in their own. Very stubborn and determined, they make it quite clear from an early age that they intend to do things their own way. These children suffer from nerves.

PISCES

Your Rising Sign

WHAT IS A RISING SIGN?
Your rising sign is the sign of the zodiac which was climbing up over the eastern horizon the moment you were born. This is not the same as your Sun sign; your Sun sign depends upon your date of birth, but your rising sign depends upon the time of day that you were born, combined with your date and place of birth.

The rising sign modifies your Sun sign character quite considerably, so when you have worked out which is your rising sign, read pages 39–40 to see how it modifies your Sun sign. Then take a deeper look by going back to 'All the Other Sun Signs' on page 21 and read the relevant Sun sign material there to discover more about your ascendant (rising sign) nature.

One final point is that the sign that is opposite your rising sign (or 'ascendant') is known as your 'descendant'. This shows what you want from other people, and it may give a clue as to your choice of friends, colleagues and lovers (see pages 41–3). So once you have found your rising sign and read the character interpretation, check out the character reading for your descendant to see what you are looking for in others.

How to Begin
Read through this section while following the example below. Even if you only have a vague idea of your birth time, you won't find this method difficult; just go for a rough time of birth and then read the Sun sign information for that sign to see if it fits your personality. If you seem to be more like the sign that comes before or after it, then it is likely that you were born a little earlier or later than your assumed time of birth. Don't forget to deduct an hour for summertime births.

1. Look at the illustration top right. You will notice that it has the time of day arranged around the outer circle. It looks a bit like a clock face, but it is different because it shows the whole 24-hour day in two-hour blocks.

2. Write the astrological symbol that represents the Sun (a circle with a dot in the middle) in the segment that corresponds to your time of birth. (If you were born during Daylight Saving or British Summer Time, deduct one hour from your birth time.) Our example shows someone who was born between 2 a.m. and 4 a.m.

PISCES

3. Now write the name of your sign or the symbol for your sign on the line which is at the end of the block of time that your Sun falls into. Our example shows a person who was born between 2 a.m. and 4 a.m. under the sign of Pisces.

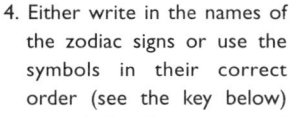

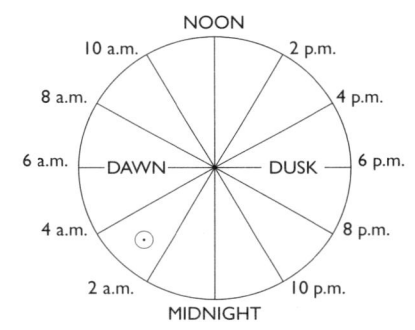

4. Either write in the names of the zodiac signs or use the symbols in their correct order (see the key below) around the chart in an anti-clockwise direction, starting from the line which is at the start of the block of time that your sun falls into.

5. The sign that appears on the left-hand side of the wheel at the 'Dawn' line is your rising sign, or ascendant. The example shows a person born with the Sun in Pisces and with Aquarius rising. Incidentally, the example chart also shows Leo, which falls on the 'Dusk' line, in the descendant. You will always find the ascendant sign on the 'Dawn' line and the descendant sign on the 'Dusk' line.

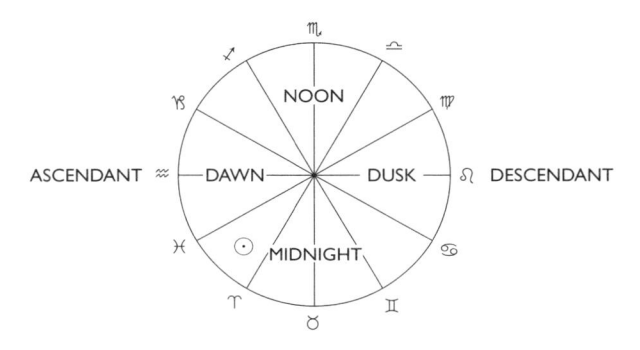

♈ Aries	♋ Cancer	♎ Libra	♑ Capricorn
♉ Taurus	♌ Leo	♏ Scorpio	♒ Aquarius
♊ Gemini	♍ Virgo	♐ Sagittarius	♓ Pisces

PISCES

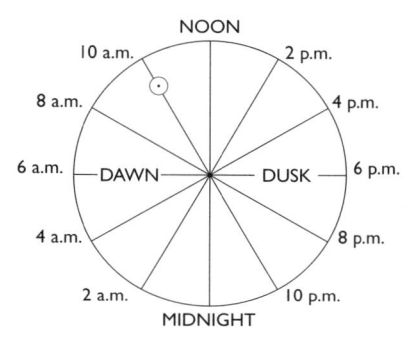

Here is another example for you to run through, just to make sure that you have grasped the idea correctly. This example is for a more awkward time of birth, being exactly on the line between two different blocks of time. This example is for a person with a Capricorn Sun sign who was born at 10 a.m.

1. The Sun is placed exactly on the 10 a.m. line.

2. The sign of Capricorn is placed on the 10 a.m. line.

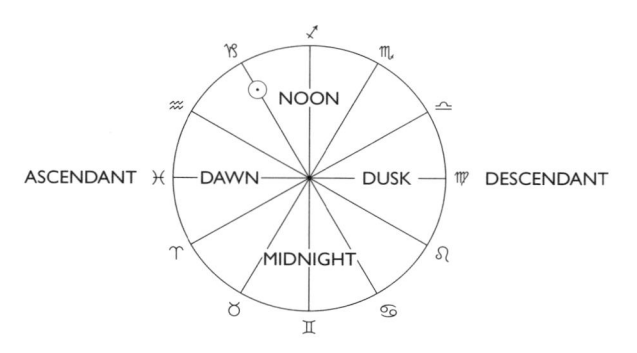

3. All the other signs are placed in astrological order (anti-clockwise) around the chart.

4. This person has the Sun in Capricorn and Pisces rising, and therefore with Virgo on the descendant.

PISCES

Using the Rising Sign Finder
Please bear in mind that this method is approximate. If you want to be really sure of your rising sign, you should contact an astrologer. However, this system will work with reasonable accuracy wherever you were born, although it would be worth checking out the Sun and ascendant combination in the following pages. You should also read the Sun sign character readings on pages 21–8 for the signs both before and after the rising sign you think is yours. This is especially important for those of you whose ascendant is right at the beginning or the end of the zodiac sign. Rising signs are such an obvious part of one's personality that one quick glance will show you which one belongs to you.

Can Your Rising Sign Tell You More about Your Future?
When it comes to tracking events, the rising sign is equal in importance to the Sun sign. So, if you want a more accurate forecast when reading newspapers or magazines, you should read the horoscope for your rising sign as well as your Sun sign. In the case of books such as this, you should really treat yourself to two: one to correspond with your rising sign, and another for your usual Sun sign, and read both each day!

How Your Rising Sign Modifies Your Sun Sign

PISCES WITH ARIES RISING You are more outgoing than the average Piscean but you can be reclusive at times. You could be very sensitive to atmospheres and even occasionally clairvoyant.

PISCES WITH TAURUS RISING You could do very well financially during your life. You are very creative and could find work in the arts, especially in the music business.

PISCES WITH GEMINI RISING You are brighter and more outgoing than most Pisceans and you could be very ambitious too. You may have felt abandoned or unloved as a child.

PISCES WITH CANCER RISING This combination makes an excellent

PISCES

teacher or counsellor. You are very sensitive, and inclined to complain to others about your problems.

PISCES WITH LEO RISING You are stubborn and determined but also a real softy with a kind heart. You could be quite clairvoyant and also artistic. You could work in music or the arts.

PISCES WITH VIRGO RISING Be careful not to lumber yourself with people who need rescuing, because they will drain you. Your early life may have been lonely or unhappy.

PISCES WITH LIBRA RISING You love beauty and may choose to work in fashion, cosmetics or something similar. You may be lazy and dreamy at times, and quite on the ball at others.

PISCES WITH SCORPIO RISING This combination makes you very psychic and keen on mysticism. You are very sensitive with deep feelings, but you may be so centred on your own needs that you sometimes forget those of others.

PISCES WITH SAGITTARIUS RISING You are quite extrovert at times, and you could feel very attracted to the spiritual life. You may travel in search of answers.

PISCES WITH CAPRICORN RISING A lonely childhood followed by a life of surprising achievement; this could be you, as long as you sustain the effort.

PISCES WITH AQUARIUS RISING You are more outgoing than the average Piscean, although still very sensitive. You could be a good astrologer or clairvoyant.

PISCES WITH PISCES RISING This is Pisces in its purest form. You are dreamy, escapist, artistic or very clairvoyant. You could work for the benefit of deprived people. You would be extremely reclusive if born after dawn, but far more outgoing and extroverted if born before.

PISCES

Pisces in Love

YOU NEED:

LOVE You can put up with almost anything as long as you know that you are with a warm-hearted, loyal and loving partner. You need romance, kindness and a deep and genuine affection.

FUN You have a wonderful sense of humour and you can bounce back from depressing circumstances reasonably easily, as long as there is something to look forward to. You enjoy outings and amusements, company and a good laugh more than most.

REASSURANCE You don't have much confidence and you need a steadfast partner who understands your need for security. Your moods may be changeable, so you need a steady, unflappable and cheerful partner.

YOU GIVE:

SYMPATHY You are a good listener and you can understand and sympathize with someone else's pain, almost to the point of feeling it yourself.

ROMANCE You never allow a relationship to become boring or mundane, and you don't forget anniversaries or birthdays. You enjoy springing pleasantly romantic surprises on your partner.

ESCAPISM You can draw a partner into your colourful fantasy world by introducing him or her to the spiritual or metaphysical side of life or simply to the inner childish world that you inhabit. Sexual fantasy could be a fertile area for your imagination, as long as you have an equally imaginative partner.

WHAT YOU CAN EXPECT FROM THE OTHER ZODIAC SIGNS:

ARIES *Truth, honesty, playfulness.* You can expect an open relationship with no hidden agendas. Your Arien lover will be childish at times, however.

TAURUS *Security, stability, comfort.* The Taurean will stand by you and try to improve your financial position. They will create a beautiful home and garden for you.

GEMINI *Stimulation, encouragement, variety.* This lover will never bore you; they give encouragement and are always ready for an outing. They give emotional support too.

CANCER *Emotional security, companionship, help.* Cancerians will never leave you stranded at a party or alone when suffering from the flu. They always lend a hand when asked.

PISCES

LEO *Affection, fun, loyalty.* Leo lovers are very steadfast and they would avenge anyone who hurt one of their family. They enjoy romping and playing affectionate love games.

VIRGO *Clear thinking, kindness, humour.* Virgoans make intelligent and amusing partners. They can be critical but are never unkind. They take their responsibility towards you seriously.

LIBRA *Fair-play, sensuality, advice.* Librans will listen to your problems and give balanced and sensible advice. They are wonderfully inventive, and are affectionate lovers too.

SCORPIO *Truth, passion, loyalty.* Scorpios will take your interests as seriously as they do their own. They will stick by you when the going gets tough and they won't flannel you.

SAGITTARIUS *Honesty, fun, novelty.* Theses lovers will never bore you and they'll keep up with whatever pace you set. They seek the truth and they don't keep their feelings hidden.

CAPRICORN *Companionship, common sense, laughter.* Capricorns enjoy doing things together and they won't leave you in the lurch when the going gets tough. They can make you laugh too.

AQUARIUS *Stimulation, friendship, sexuality.* Aquarians are friends as well as lovers. They are great fun because you never know what they are going to do next, in or out of bed.

WHICH SIGN ARE YOU COMPATIBLE WITH?

PISCES/ARIES
Aries could be too pushy for Pisces but they may share interests.

PISCES/TAURUS
Shared interests and sensual natures can make this very good.

PISCES/GEMINI
Shared sense of humour and love of life makes this a good combination.

PISCES/CANCER
An excellent match, so long as neither is too dependent.

PISCES/LEO
Probably better for work than love, but nonetheless all right.

PISCES/VIRGO
With give and take on both sides this can work well.

PISCES/LIBRA
Good sexual rapport but otherwise disappointing.

PISCES/SCORPIO
As long as the Scorpio is very loving, this can work well.

PISCES

PISCES/SAGITTARIUS
Can work well, both love children, travel and freedom.

PISCES/CAPRICORN
Very little in common, could be an attraction of opposites.

PISCES/AQUARIUS
Neither very practical but should get on well in many ways.

PISCES/PISCES
Same signs can be too similar, but this can often be very successful.

Your Prospects for 1999

LOVE

It looks as though you will have a much happier and more successful year as far as love and romance go this year than has been the case for some years past. If you are single and in the market for a light-hearted romance or two, there should be nothing to spoil this dream. The only really difficult time is likely to come in mid-August when misunderstandings could suddenly arise. If you are looking for a settled partnership this year, your chances of finding it are really rather good. Venus spends a fair bit of time in your opposite sign during July and August and then again during October and November and this should bring you the kind of love relationship that you most want. In addition to this, Mars will add a passionate and sexual aspect to any romance for you both at the very beginning of the year and again from mid-May to mid-July. However, there may be a setback or two during May and June and it would be worth waiting until after the 4th of June before making any important plans for the future. If you need to talk things over with a lover, then September and October will be the best months for getting this done while May and the run up to the end of the year could be difficult times for any form of sensible communication between you. Having said all this, this should be a relatively easy and successful year for all personal and business relationships or partnerships.

MONEY AND WORK

Your business and your job appears to be the least settled and easy area of your life this year. There may be little more than a move of premises to cope with but even that will be disrupting and dislocating for a while but it may be hard to communicate with those around you at times too this year, especially during the second half of July when Mercury is in retrograde

PISCES

motion. A very easy and successful period during June could be followed by any amount of setbacks during July and August. If you are expecting a rise in pay at this time, it is unlikely to come your way. Oddly enough, despite this you will have opportunities to achieve some of your greatest ambitions during the latter part of 1999. Financially speaking, there may be windfalls and other forms of gain and advantage at almost any time this year and the chances are that you will be able to set up savings schemes and other forms of security for the future now. There may be a few financial problems that have been left over from the past right at the start of the year but the outlook from mid-February onwards is really rather good.

HEALTH

You will have to guard against one or two problems this year, especially during July when a cold could lay you really low. From mid-August to mid-September you will have to watch what you eat, either because you would find it all too easy to gain weight at that time or because your stomach or your system may be more sensitive than is usual. Sudden and unexpected ailments may descend upon you this year but the chances are that they will eventually vanish once again just as suddenly. Your family and your loved ones seem to be pretty fit with the exception of older male relatives who may have to cope with some illness during the middle part of the year. Be careful if you have any heavy lifting to do during March and April, because you might just strain your shoulders or the upper part of your back. Other than these rather vague problems, you should be pretty fit for most of the year and anything that does blow up will subside down again just as quickly

FAMILY AND HOME

Older male family members may be ill at times this year, especially between May and October but other than this, there shouldn't be too much trouble. You are more likely to find that work colleagues fall sick than any member of your family. Your improved financial position may prompt you to move house or to renovate the one you are living in but this will be a matter of personal choice because there will be no real pressure on you to move. On the contrary, you are more likely to happily work on your garden or to make small alterations and improvements around the house than to make a major move now.

LUCK

You could find some real bargains this year and if you collect valuable items of any kind, you could find that some of these come your way by sheer good luck. This should be a good year for money luck and it would be worth trying a small wager here and there as this should pay off quite well for you. May and June look like being great months for fun and amusements and a holiday or a break of any kind at that time would be extremely enjoyable.

The Aspects and their Astrological Meanings

CONJUNCT	This shows important events which are usually, but not always, good.
SEXTILE	Good, particularly for work and mental activity.
SQUARE	Difficult, challenging.
TRINE	Great for romance, family life and creativity.
OPPOSITE	Awkward, depressing, challenging.
INTO	This shows when a particular planet enters a new sign of the zodiac, thus setting off a new phase or a new set of circumstances.
DIRECT	When a planet resumes normal direct motion.
RETROGRADE	When a planet apparently begins to go backwards.
VOID	When the Moon makes no aspect to any planet.

PISCES

September at a Glance

LOVE	♥	♥	♥	♥	
WORK	★	★	★		
MONEY	£				
HEALTH	✪	✪	✪	✪	✪
LUCK	♘	♘			

TUESDAY, 1ST SEPTEMBER
Moon trine Saturn

You'll be in a serious frame of mind today, with no time for frivolous gossip or idle people. You'll be busy thinking of intellectual matters, and may be planning a celebration that will take a lot of organizing.

WEDNESDAY, 2ND SEPTEMBER
Void Moon

The term 'void of course' means that neither the Moon nor any of the other planets is making any important aspects to anything else today. When this kind of day occurs, the worst thing you can do is to try and start something new or to get anything important off the ground. Do nothing special today except for routine tasks

THURSDAY, 3RD SEPTEMBER
Moon conjunct Neptune

The sensitivities of your friends will surprise you because you won't expect them to be so mindful of your feelings. Tender affection is the key to happiness as your emotions are fragile. A nice dinner party, a romantic movie or a snuggle with a loved one should be the order of the evening

FRIDAY, 4TH SEPTEMBER
Mars opposite Uranus

Anything could happen today, and none of it is likely to please you. The last thing you want is a surprise as you'd like your routine to remain exactly as it is. However, something is bound to disrupt it. Try to make the best of whatever happens!

PISCES

SATURDAY, 5TH SEPTEMBER
Moon opposite Venus

Ladies can expect one of those days today. Your hormones may be travelling in the wrong direction and your mood may be tense and tetchy for no real reason as a result of this. Both sexes could be feeling a bit off-colour

SUNDAY, 6TH SEPTEMBER
Full Moon eclipse

All close personal affairs need some scrutiny as the lunar eclipse casts a shadow on your expectations in a relationship. Changes are inevitable, perhaps only surface ones, but any differences must be aired now if you want a healthy relationship in the future

MONDAY, 7TH SEPTEMBER
Moon sextile Neptune

You've had enough of media hype and will want to indulge in something quite highbrow and worthwhile. If you can share a visit to a concert, theatrical performance or a museum with a friend, so much the better

TUESDAY, 8TH SEPTEMBER
Mercury into Virgo

Mercury moves into your Solar seventh house of relationships, emphasizing your dealings with others. This would be a good time to get together with others for practical reasons and it's a wonderful time to start a new relationship with someone special. If you need to put the romance back into your marriage or communicate your feelings to a lover, then do so now

WEDNESDAY, 9TH SEPTEMBER
Mercury trine Saturn

A serious talk with a loved one will go a long way to restoring understanding between you. A rift may have developed simply because you didn't want to talk about your fears and anxieties. A problem shared is a problem halved

THURSDAY, 10TH SEPTEMBER
Venus trine Saturn

The aspect between Venus and Saturn denotes a make-or-break time in a relationship. It may be that you've passed the stage of airy romanticism and will be considering the pro's and con's of continuing a relationship. Whatever your decision, it could change your life

PISCES

FRIDAY, 11TH SEPTEMBER
Mercury conjunct Venus

Words of love will be flowing all around you. Your lover may surprise you by suggesting a romantic evening out or by bringing you tickets to a show, a musical, or a sporting event. You should make the most of this romantic communication.

SATURDAY, 12TH SEPTEMBER
Moon sextile Mars

An energetic time for you as you marshal your forces, get family members into action and prepare an ambitious plan for redecoration, or even a house move. You'll demand that everyone pulls their weight but make sure that you do, too. Standing about and bellowing orders won't be very helpful!

SUNDAY, 13TH SEPTEMBER
Moon square Jupiter

It's a highly nostalgic day, and you will want to enjoy a quiet moment reflecting on times gone by. Souvenirs, mementoes, old photos or even a snatch of familiar music will evoke memories. We all need some time to look at where we've been. That way, we see how far we've come.

MONDAY, 14TH SEPTEMBER
Moon sextile Venus

Give yourself over to absolute pleasure! The lunar aspect of Venus puts you in a sensual mood, determined to enjoy the finer things of life. Good food, good wines and the company of someone you love is the recipe for perfect bliss. It doesn't matter what you do, as long as you enjoy it.

TUESDAY, 15TH SEPTEMBER
Moon sextile Sun

This is a time for togetherness and romance. The two great luminaries, the Sun and Moon, cast a golden light on affairs of the heart and promise a pleasurable interlude away from the hustle and bustle of daily life.

WEDNESDAY, 16TH SEPTEMBER
Sun opposite Jupiter

This is one of those days when optimism can be a fault. It's all very well being positive about your future, but there does have to be some grounding in reality for your wishes to come true. Don't be tempted to make far-reaching plans without consulting your other half or you could find your fond dreams quickly evaporating.

PISCES

THURSDAY, 17TH SEPTEMBER
Moon conjunct Mars

If you need to get a few chores out of the way, then do them today. Mars will give you the energy you need to put your back into whatever you have to accomplish, so give full attention to major projects and career matters.

FRIDAY, 18TH SEPTEMBER
Moon trine Saturn

There's no doubt that you've been too busy to let your other half in on everything you're doing. However, today there's a chance to alleviate all suspicions by coming out into the open. It's important to remember that sharing the burden is half-way to finding a solution.

SATURDAY, 19TH SEPTEMBER
Mercury opposite Jupiter

Guard your tongue and take care not to become upset at someone else's tactless remarks. Your partner may be restless and in need of a change, so you could soon find yourself booking up a last-minute holiday.

SUNDAY, 20TH SEPTEMBER
New Moon

Just carry on as usual and deny yourself nothing! The New Moon suggests that you take a fresh look at your partnerships and relationships, whether personal or professional.

MONDAY, 21ST SEPTEMBER
Moon sextile Pluto

Someone could be looking out for you or even doing a bit of real spying on your behalf. Inside information will come your way and this could have wonderful implications for your career or for any kind of aspiration that you have. Your sex life could take off like a rocket due to your partner's renewed enthusiasm or, if you are single, a new amour is on the way now.

TUESDAY, 22ND SEPTEMBER
Sun trine Neptune

This is an inspired day on which you'll receive all the encouragement you need from your friends and the person who loves you most. Don't be afraid to express your creative thoughts and talents. Your efforts will be well received.

PISCES

WEDNESDAY, 23RD SEPTEMBER
Sun into Libra

A highly passionate phase in your life begins with the Sun's entry into your area of sexuality, shared resources and physical attraction. You'll get further if you are direct and to the point, so discuss any intimate problem that worries you with someone you trust to relieve anxieties. Your finances should also improve within the next month, in the form of a windfall or by a more sensible use of your savings bringing a greater return on investments.

THURSDAY, 24TH SEPTEMBER
Mercury into Libra

Secrets must be kept, that's the astral message of Mercury entering your Solar house of intimate affairs. If you are involved in a clandestine relationship you had better make sure that your personal security code isn't breached. Confidences of all sorts, whether sexual or financial must be guarded since it's all too easy to slip up!

FRIDAY, 25TH SEPTEMBER
Sun conjunct Mercury

You should be very shrewd today. The Sun lights up Mercury giving you the capacity to sort through difficult financial dealings and to cope with all sorts of forms and officials. Nothing will get past your keen gaze now!

SATURDAY, 26TH SEPTEMBER
Moon conjunct Pluto

Think deeply about where your life is leading and where you would like to go. Don't get side-tracked by minor details or by having to do things for others that they could easily do for themselves. At work, try delegating for a change or allowing your colleagues to carry their own responsibilities rather than leaving the gutsy jobs to you.

SUNDAY, 27TH SEPTEMBER
Mercury sextile Pluto

You are at your subtle best today. You know that the direct approach is not going to work with anything that smacks of officialdom. Fortunately you are cunning enough to use the roundabout route to get what you want.

MONDAY, 28TH SEPTEMBER
Moon trine Saturn

It's good to have supportive friends. When you are anxious a few wise words

PISCES

from an experienced person can set your mind at rest. Be open about your aims, ambitions and fears and you'll find that those around you will offer help and friendly advice.

TUESDAY, 29TH SEPTEMBER
Sun sextile Pluto

This is a chance to show off your leadership qualities. People at work will look to you for guidance, but it may not be wise to reveal all that you know! Financially, things are looking better with the chance of profit in the offing. However, discretion is important here too.

WEDNESDAY, 30TH SEPTEMBER
Venus into Libra

Your mood may become slightly awkward and possessive over the next month or so, but outwardly you will endeavour to keep the peace and appear to be full of sweetness and light. This could be a good strategy, but you will probably have to dig in your heels at some point and send out clear signals to show everyone concerned that you mean business.

October at a Glance

LOVE	♥	♥	♥	
WORK	★	★	★	★
MONEY	£	£		
HEALTH	✛			
LUCK	♘	♘		

THURSDAY, 1ST OCTOBER
Sun trine Uranus

You could be in for a spot of luck in some of the more important areas of your life. Business matters could suddenly bring the financial results that you need, while loving relationships will begin to work the way you want. Business or personal partnerships will be helped by a change in circumstances. This may seem to help your partner more than you, but it will benefit you too.

PISCES

FRIDAY, 2ND OCTOBER
Moon opposite Mars

There's a dose of the blues today, with very little raising your enthusiasm or attracting your interest. Possibly you have a nagging worry that won't let you to take a more positive view of your situation. You may be letting the disappointments and frustrations you've experienced at work cast a cloud over your life. Try to perk yourself up, for every cloud has a silver lining.

SATURDAY, 3RD OCTOBER
Moon square Pluto

You may feel that you are being pushed or manipulated into a position which doesn't suit you. You know your own worth and you are not about to have it minimized by others. If you feel that you're being treated unfairly by those around you, you are liable to lose your temper with them today. Pour out your troubles to an understanding friend.

SUNDAY, 4TH OCTOBER
Moon conjunct Jupiter

You will have the opportunity to express your most deeply held views and beliefs today. You seem to be looking for a change in lifestyle that will allow you more space and opportunity to be yourself. The planets seem to suggest that this is just what you will soon get.

MONDAY, 5TH OCTOBER
Venus sextile Pluto

You will have rather mixed fortunes today. On the one hand, your personal life and relationship with loved ones will be pleasant and peaceful. You and your lover will enjoy each other's company and may even go out for a meal or a minor celebration of some kind. However, there could be a few tense moments with a figure in authority or even a government department.

TUESDAY, 6TH OCTOBER
Full Moon

The Full Moon shows that you're at a turning point in dealing with finances. Turn your attention to creating a far more orderly and efficient way of managing your resources. Take a look at savings schemes that will give a good return on your investments. It's important that you don't take anything for granted, so dig out your accounts, prune expenses savagely and make the most of financial opportunities.

PISCES

WEDNESDAY, 7TH OCTOBER
Mars into Virgo

With the entry of Mars into your opposite sign there's a small rumbling of discontent within a close relationship. You may feel the need for extra independence and freedom from restrictions so if your partner is possessive, the new assertive may come as something of a shock. There may be an element of envy emerging, and by that we mean one partner unconsciously competing against the other. As long as you remember that you're actually part of a team, things shouldn't go too far astray.

THURSDAY, 8TH OCTOBER
Moon sextile Jupiter

You're in a very good mood today as the mixed rays of Jupiter and the Moon make you outgoing and open-minded. You're in the mood for fun so involve yourself in a get-together with your friends. You may find yourself cast as a go-between, carrying a message from one person to another. Do this task well, because a lot depends on it and you'll certainly win gratitude.

FRIDAY, 9TH OCTOBER
Moon trine Uranus

There seems to be a number unexpected events going on in and around your home and family. There could be news of a family celebration or even an unusual reconciliation of some kind. If you have done good turns for relatives in the past, these could now be paid back to you. You may also find an interesting item for your home.

SATURDAY, 10TH OCTOBER
Mars trine Saturn

Actions speak louder than words to a loved one today. If these actions are well thought out and have a grounding in common sense, they're bound to win approval.

SUNDAY, 11TH OCTOBER
Neptune direct

You may have felt badly let down recently and prone to questioning your basic ideals. From today though, Neptune moves forward once more which will help renew your faith in human nature over the coming months. It should be easier to maintain a positive mental attitude from now on. You may even experience meaningful or predictive dreams.

PISCES

MONDAY, 12TH OCTOBER
Mercury into Scorpio

Mercury enters the most philosophical area of your chart giving you a chance to grow mentally. Many of your past beliefs will fall by the wayside as you find other concepts that fit more logically into your life. Positive thinking is important since you'll realize that only negativity has held you back. The academically inclined should do well under this influence. Mercury also boosts your travel prospects.

TUESDAY, 13TH OCTOBER
Moon square Mercury

You must watch your health today and take care not to have any kind of silly accident. This is not the best day to play sports, go horseback riding or take any chances. Rest and relax and try to allow your rather jangled nerves to settle before doing anything important. Someone at work may get you down today, and you'll have a strong desire to escape!

WEDNESDAY, 14TH OCTOBER
Mercury sextile Mars

Your partner could surprise you with a plan for an impromptu trip. If you are very lucky you will find yourself whisked off for a short break full of luxury and passion! Even with a little less fortune, you will still have an excellent time in the company of those who mean most to you.

THURSDAY, 15TH OCTOBER
Moon trine Saturn

There's no doubt that you've been too busy to spend enough time with your partner. This could be the reason for you bottling up a problem which has been bothering you. Come clean and you'll get all the support you need.

FRIDAY, 16TH OCTOBER
Moon square Pluto

With the Moon and Pluto in an awkward aspect it may be a difficult day to deal with bosses or your partner. You have to remember that those around you have worries too, so don't be too offended if they seem cool and distant.

SATURDAY, 17TH OCTOBER
Mercury square Uranus

It's very likely that you'll take on too much today. You may feel your conscience pricking and this will spur you on to overload your schedule. Nervous tension is likely, so try to take things easy or at least one at a time.

PISCES

SUNDAY, 18TH OCTOBER
Uranus direct

If you have been confused, unsure of yourself or even plain crazy lately, you should be able to get your brain into gear once again. Uranus is moving to direct motion and this will clear your mind and bring you far more opportunities than you have had of late. This planetary movement will end that feeling of being in limbo.

MONDAY, 19TH OCTOBER
Mars square Pluto

In total contrast to yesterday's gentle stars, the explosive combination of Mars and Pluto makes you edgy and prone to anxiety. You are very sensitive to negative vibes, and the irrational emotions of others are disruptive to your mood. You may find that someone else's jealousy is at the root of the problem. Try not to overreact, and don't allow yourself to be caught up in a destructive cycle of tit for tat.

TUESDAY, 20TH OCTOBER
New Moon

Today's New Moon forecasts a new start in one of the most intimate areas of your horoscope. It's a chance to review your personal life and expectations. Past emotional hurts can be put behind you now, giving you room to look to the future with more confidence. Financial affairs also come under scrutiny because you're in the right frame of mind to sort out any muddle.

WEDNESDAY, 21ST OCTOBER
Moon square Uranus

The safe confines of your home and the daily routine are quite suffocating at the moment as the aspect between the Moon and Uranus gives you a taste for freedom. Assert your independence today and cast off all unnecessary restrictions. Your quest for adventure might not get you far, but a change is as good as a rest.

THURSDAY, 22ND OCTOBER
Sun square Neptune

This could be a muddled day on which you don't know quite what to believe. There seems to be someone trying to pull the wool over your eyes, probably in connection with a money matter. Sit down quietly and try to plan your next move.

FRIDAY, 23RD OCTOBER
Sun into Scorpio

The Sun moves into your house of philosophy, beliefs and travel today indicating

PISCES

that the next month will expand your mental and physical horizons enormously. This area of the horoscope is associated with adventure and journeys to distant and exotic parts of the world. Tempting as that idea may seem, the truth is likely to be closer to home. It's a time to indulge your curiosity, so you'll embark on a journey within your own mind and explore a religious or spiritual dimension. You may wish to enter a more academic field. Examine the possibilities of college courses and other forms of adult education.

SATURDAY, 24TH OCTOBER
Venus into Scorpio

Everything seems a bit dull and mundane to you to today and your restless mood will make you yearn to visit far-flung places. If your lover suggests that you start planning a trip, you will jump at the idea and practical matters such as time and money will be beside the point.

SUNDAY, 25TH OCTOBER
Saturn into Aries retrograde

Saturn returns to your area of money and possessions today showing a tightening of the wallet and possibly a couple of unwelcome bills landing on your doorstep. Don't panic! You will sort these out even if you have to ask for more time to do so.

MONDAY, 26TH OCTOBER
Sun conjunct Venus

What a wonderful day to fall in love! If you are smitten by Cupid's arrow, the chances are that the object of your desires will be a fascinating foreigner or a captivating stranger. The good news is that the love of your life will feel as equally over the Moon about you!

TUESDAY, 27TH OCTOBER
Moon sextile Mercury

There may be a sudden opportunity today for getting away from it all. This could be a short and interesting journey, or possibly something far more involved and distant. You will make contact with people who are some distance from you and you may even receive an invitation to visit them. The chances are that the people in question are either relatives or ex-neighbours.

WEDNESDAY, 28TH OCTOBER
Moon square Sun

It's a fairly mixed-up day emotionally speaking, as you feel somewhat vulnerable and

PISCES

not your usual outgoing self. Although the trends are generally good, you can't quite believe your luck and will be waiting for something to go wrong. You may also have a vague suspicion about a friend's motives, but don't do anything about it just yet.

THURSDAY, 29TH OCTOBER
Saturn square Neptune

It's a moody outlook for you especially since financial pressures seem to be extra heavy at the moment. You are painfully aware that money doesn't grow on trees, so a sponging acquaintance will get short shrift!

FRIDAY, 30TH OCTOBER
Moon sextile Saturn

Older people or those in positions of responsibility will be on hand with help and advice today. You may need to review your finances, working out a sensible budget for the future. You will receive thanks from others for your past efforts and you may even receive some kind of extra recognition from your superiors and your colleagues at work.

SATURDAY, 31ST OCTOBER
Moon conjunct Jupiter

Luck takes a turn for the better as the Moon meets up with Jupiter in your house of personality. You'll feel happier, believing that everything will work out all right in the end. If you are on the move you will particularly benefit from this exuberant planetary influence, since Jupiter governs long-distance travellers. Good chances occur again and again today, so don't look a gift horse in the mouth.

November at a Glance

LOVE	♥	♥	♥	♥	♥
WORK	★				
MONEY	£	£	£		
HEALTH	☥				
LUCK	♘	♘	♘	♘	

PISCES

SUNDAY, 1ST NOVEMBER
Mercury into Sagittarius

Mercury enters your Solar tenth house of aims and ambitions today. You can keep your eye firmly on your goals and know that you have a fair chance of achieving them with some constructive thinking and planning.

MONDAY, 2ND NOVEMBER
Void Moon

There are no important planetary aspects today and even the Moon is unaspected. This kind of a day is called a 'void of course Moon' day, because the Moon has no aspects during this part of its course. The best way to approach such a day is to do what is normal and natural for you without starting anything new or particularly special.

TUESDAY, 3RD NOVEMBER
Moon square Neptune

This is not a day to sign on the dotted line. Don't take out any hire-purchase agreements or sign yourself up to some fly-by-night scheme that promises high financial returns. It'll turn out to be nothing more than a cheap con trick. Be sensible and leave all money matters for another day.

WEDNESDAY, 4TH NOVEMBER
Full Moon

The Full Moon puts the spotlight on your intellect and capabilities. You may feel a desire to improve your qualifications, if so then this is the perfect time to find out more about available courses in your area. On the other hand, you may find yourself questioning your aspirations and convictions. Mentally this is a challenging time, but remember that you're never too old to learn something new.

THURSDAY, 5TH NOVEMBER
Moon trine Neptune

The theme of aspirations continues today as you think deeply about what you should set your sights on. It's becoming obvious that you've already achieved many objectives, while others don't hold the appeal that they once did. Talk things over with friends and you'll find new ambitions to replace the old.

FRIDAY, 6TH NOVEMBER
Mercury conjunct Pluto

You'll find yourself in a very influential position today and the combined energies of Mercury and Pluto make you a force to be reckoned with. However, there are

PISCES

ways and means of wielding your power, and nagging isn't the best one. It is easier to get your own way by subtle persuasion than outright confrontation!

SATURDAY, 7TH NOVEMBER
Mars opposite Jupiter

You could be up against a lot of opposition from others today but you'll be well aware of their intentions and motives, so there will be nothing going on behind your back. You may need to put your foot down over a money matter.

SUNDAY, 8TH NOVEMBER
Venus trine Jupiter

There's a fortunate flavour in today's stars. Jupiter and Venus combine to assert a positive influence on everything connected with knowledge, education and travel. Your social life will also be affected by this splendid astral pairing, so circulate and you'll find more like-minded people than you thought possible. Opportunities for new friendships, and possibly even a new job, are not out of the question.

MONDAY, 9TH NOVEMBER
Venus sextile Mars

Strong physical attractions are the order of the day as Venus gets to grips with Mars. In short, you'll be feeling sensuous and particularly prone to exotic fantasies. Even better, you will probably get the chance to put some of them into practice!

TUESDAY, 10TH NOVEMBER
Sun trine Jupiter

If you have had to delay or put off a journey, you will now be able to go ahead with it. You may be on the receiving end of a small windfall or you could buy a winning ticket in some kind of raffle.

WEDNESDAY, 11TH NOVEMBER
Moon square Venus

Thoughts of love occupy your every moment, or would do if you had the leisure to enjoy them. Unfortunately you'll have little peace today as the pressures of work will tear you away from more pleasurable activities. At least you can offset the boredom of your duties by playing music to take your mind off the here-and-now.

THURSDAY, 12TH NOVEMBER
Moon square Pluto

There seems to be too many demands being put on you at the moment. Your

PISCES

partner may be keen to tell you where your duties lie, while your job is demanding too much of your time and energy. Look closely at both these situations and work out a reasonable break-down of your time ... remembering to leave some time for yourself.

FRIDAY, 13TH NOVEMBER
Jupiter direct

This is an important time for you because things that you have been planning and working towards are beginning to come to fruition. Use the positive traits of your personality help things move forward.

SATURDAY, 14TH NOVEMBER
Sun sextile Mars

This should be an action-packed day as you whisk your other half away to an impromptu social event. If you haven't got another half, you might find one at a gathering of friends.

SUNDAY, 15TH NOVEMBER
Moon sextile Mercury

You won't stand for people who hold forth about things they don't understand, and you won't be able to resist putting them in their place. In meetings, social or professional you'll be able to put your point of view across clearly. There's no doubt that others will listen as you are obviously well informed and concise in your argument.

MONDAY, 16TH NOVEMBER
Moon opposite Saturn

If money affairs have got you down, take heart. The influence of the planet Saturn can show you a way out of present difficulties. It may not be easy and could require a lot of thought, but it's possible to improve your financial situation.

TUESDAY, 17TH NOVEMBER
Venus into Sagittarius

A woman could be instrumental in helping you to achieve one of your dearest ambitions quite out of the blue. This friend or colleague will put herself out for no other reason than to help you on your way. A sudden and unexpected social invitation could come through work and this is so favourable that you really must accept.

PISCES

WEDNESDAY, 18TH NOVEMBER
Moon trine Jupiter

Travel is on your mind today, the further away your destination, the better! If you are extra lucky you could be jetting off to the sun, but if not plan a trip for the not-too-distant future!

THURSDAY, 19TH NOVEMBER
New Moon

Today's New Moon certainly indicates a new start for you. You're filled to the brim with good ideas, and your mind is working overtime bringing you close to genius level. If there's a subject that has interested you for some time, this could be your chance to learn more and possibly gain a qualification. Anything that increases your knowledge and experience is in favour at the moment and a stimulating conversation will point the way forward.

FRIDAY, 20TH NOVEMBER
Mercury square Jupiter

Don't take too much on face value today. It's unwise to base your opinions of a person on gossip because it's likely that the information you have is misleading, if not slanderous! Keep an open mind and only rely on sources that are above reproach. Even then it is worth double-checking, because anyone can make a mistake. Over-optimism is a factor to be watched too. Try to remain realistic on this confusing day.

SATURDAY, 21ST NOVEMBER
Mercury retrograde

Mercury turns to retrograde motion today in the area of your chart that is devoted to aims and ambitions. This will delay your progress for a little while, making it hard for you to cope with the amount of pressure that is being put on you. An older person or someone in a position of authority may decide to hurt you by using sarcasm or by holding you up to ridicule.

SUNDAY, 22ND NOVEMBER
Sun into Sagittarius

Career affairs are in the spotlight so concentrate on where you are going and make an effort to impress the right people over the next few weeks. Forget about romance for a while and concentrate on business and financial goals instead.

PISCES

MONDAY, 23RD NOVEMBER
Venus conjunct Pluto

Venus is in conjunction with Pluto showing that feelings run high. You are likely to get obsessive over something and won't take no for an answer. In career affairs especially there's a determination to go right to the top. However, in affairs of the heart this conjunction raises your emotions to almost fanatical levels. Take care!

TUESDAY, 24TH NOVEMBER
Moon sextile Sun

The Sun and Moon link in a positive aspect and your mood is calm. You seem content to go along with what others want and fortunately they seem to want much the same as you do, so there shouldn't be any conflict of interest.

WEDNESDAY, 25TH NOVEMBER
Venus sextile Uranus

Luck is due unexpectedly today. This could occur in work where your originality will be admired, or as a sudden, overwhelming attraction to someone who walks into your life. This mystery person will have a profound effect on your emotions.

THURSDAY, 26TH NOVEMBER
Moon sextile Saturn

This is a great time to start some kind of savings arrangement. This may be something long term such as a pension scheme, or as short term as putting your small change into a coffee jar. It doesn't matter whether it is large or small, it will all work to your benefit in the future. Your parents may help you out, but if it is you who helps them it will be appreciated

FRIDAY, 27TH NOVEMBER
Neptune into Aquarius

Neptune, the misty planet of inspiration, enters the most secretive area of your chart from today. This long-awaited movement will enhance your already powerful intuition and could lead to some spectacular psychic experiences.

SATURDAY, 28TH NOVEMBER
Mars trine Neptune

This is a marvellous time to show that your feelings of affection run strong and true. You're in the mood for fun with your partner and any friends who happen to drop by. A perfect day!

PISCES

SUNDAY, 29TH NOVEMBER
Sun conjunct Pluto

In career affairs you are about to be thrust into prominence. This may not mean the limelight, but a responsibility placed on your shoulders that only you can carry. You have all the knowledge, experience and determination to carry this task through to a successful conclusion. This could transform your working life and earn you the rewards you justly deserve.

MONDAY, 30TH NOVEMBER
Moon conjunct Saturn

If another depressing envelope arrives on the mat this morning, adding to the pile of bills that you already have, then it is obviously time to take some kind of action. It may be worth seeing if you can reschedule debts, obtain loans or grants or even call in loans that you have dished out to others when your finances were healthier.

December at a Glance

LOVE	♥		
WORK	★	★	★
MONEY	£	£	£
HEALTH	✚		
LUCK	♘	♘	♘

TUESDAY, 1ST DECEMBER
Mercury sextile Uranus

You are a walking, talking brain-box today! Mercury and Uranus cause your IQ levels to soar! However, in career affairs and with any ambitions it'll be important to keep tight-lipped about some of your stunning plans.

WEDNESDAY, 2ND DECEMBER
Sun sextile Uranus

A crusading zeal grips you and you'll be eager to change everything from your working practices to the world at large. You won't tolerate injustice or tyrannical attitudes from anyone and you'll be prepared to stand up for your rights!

PISCES

THURSDAY, 3RD DECEMBER
Full Moon

The Full Moon puts the spotlight on your career. There have been a lot of changes internally and around you. You have to decide exactly what you want, and in which direction you should go. Before you can act you need a good plan, so take time to make sure that your strategies for progress are workable. Employers and authority figures will be impressed by your drive and determination.

FRIDAY, 4TH DECEMBER
Moon opposite Venus

There's a see-saw of priorities today as the Moon opposes Venus, bringing a crisis of conscience. There's plenty you should be doing in your professional life, but there are family commitments that have to be fulfilled as well. Your heart lies with the more personal side of your life but there are some duties that you simply can't shirk. Make the best of this because you can't win on both counts at once.

SATURDAY, 5TH DECEMBER
Mercury sextile Mars

You'll find yourself in a very decisive frame of mind today. You're in a go-getting, high-achieving mood, capable of anything and secure against all that the world throws at you. There will be some who may criticize, but their words will be like water off a duck's back!

SUNDAY, 6TH DECEMBER
Moon trine Jupiter

Today should be notable for fun and good humour. The Moon makes an excellent aspect to Jupiter encouraging you to enjoy your own talents. You may feel like expressing yourself artistically, or embark on a devil-may-care course of romantic enjoyment. If you have children, you'll have cause to feel proud of their achievements.

MONDAY, 7TH DECEMBER
Moon sextile Mars

This is a good day to be at work because anything to do with chores and duties is likely to be very successful. Home-based projects will go well today too, so get down to the ironing or clean out the garage, because you will feel all the better for doing so.

PISCES

TUESDAY, 8TH DECEMBER
Moon trine Sun

We'll happily ignore the ill-omened reputation of the day because the Moon is in excellent aspect to the Sun which both adds to your physical vitality and opens career opportunities. You could cope with anything and win through with ease. You're in tune with yourself, your goals are clear and you'll be able to achieve them with time to spare.

WEDNESDAY, 9TH DECEMBER
Venus trine Saturn

There's likely to be something of lasting value coming your way. This may be a gift or a reward for past services, cash or something that you will treasure forever. Whatever the nature of your gain, you will be very pleased with it.

THURSDAY, 10TH DECEMBER
Moon square Sun

You may be feeling a bit downhearted or over-sensitive and your partner has only to say 'hello' for you to jump down his or her throat. Try to relax and do whatever calms you down. Maybe try a bit of meditation, or take the dog for a walk, listen to some nice music or chat to a friend on the phone. Later in the day, a pleasant surprise will lift your mood and make you feel that the sun is shining again.

FRIDAY, 11TH DECEMBER
Venus into Capricorn

Venus, planet of harmony, enters your Solar area of friendships from today starting a period of social activities, fun and new encounters. Romance and social life mingle now, so at the least this will be a month of flirtation. An old friend may also be seen in a new and more intimate light. If you have any artistic aspirations, you should follow your instincts because the influence of Venus is excellent for anything that shows flair and originality.

SATURDAY, 12TH DECEMBER
Mars sextile Pluto

It's a great day for the ambitious because there's a chance of career advancement. If you run your own business you will find that swift action is the key to success. Your personal initiative will be the power behind you today.

PISCES

SUNDAY, 13TH DECEMBER
Moon sextile Sun

New work prospects are in the offing and your ambitions are running high, so go for it! Changes in your career will benefit you ultimately, and you could end up making a considerable profit in the near future.

MONDAY, 14TH DECEMBER
Moon sextile Venus

Your partner may surprise you by giving you an unexpected welcome home. He or she may have the washing done, the dinner in the oven, a bottle of wine cooling in the fridge and a warm smile on his or her face. There may be good news which helps you both towards achieving a shared goal. A woman could be helpful and even inspirational in connection with work.

TUESDAY, 15TH DECEMBER
Mars trine Uranus

With Mars linking with Uranus the chance of an unexpected tryst is on the cards on this amorous day. Your passions are aroused and if there's a hint of intrigue involved, you'll be in your element.

WEDNESDAY, 16TH DECEMBER
Moon sextile Neptune

There's nothing you'd like better than to cast aside all your mundane cares and whisk yourself away on a holiday. If you can't manage that at the moment, at least give yourself an outing, preferably with someone you really like.

THURSDAY, 17TH DECEMBER
Moon sextile Uranus

You should have a lucky break in connection with your job. If you don't work, or if work is not your first priority, then something good will happen which helps you reach your personal goals. Something may come to light that has been hidden from view until now.

FRIDAY, 18TH DECEMBER
New Moon

Your career gets a kick-start from the New Moon today. For many this heralds the start of a new job, for others a chance to branch out on your own. Good luck!

PISCES

SATURDAY, 19TH DECEMBER
Sun trine Saturn

Pure practicality is your main strength today. In career and financial affairs, your slow steady progress is to be admired. A methodical approach to problems will result in eventual success in any venture.

SUNDAY, 20TH DECEMBER
Moon square Mars

You may be under economic pressure but some people around you are convinced that you're made of money, and equally keen to spend it. It doesn't matter how much you protest that you can't really afford too many treats you just won't be believed. It's time to take some radical action and put your foot down firmly. Refuse to part with cash because apart from the financial loss, it'll cause long-term resentment on your part.

MONDAY, 21ST DECEMBER
Mercury conjunct Pluto

You are the most persuasive person around today. The clarity and power of your arguments will sway the most stubborn person around to your way of thinking. In all career affairs, the ladder of success leads you onward and upward.

TUESDAY, 22ND DECEMBER
Sun into Capricorn

The Sun's progress into your Solar area of hopes, wishes and ideals shows that the ball's in your court. You have all the facts at your disposal, you've thought your prospects through and now it's up to you to make your desires come true. There are risks, but if you really want something then you'd better start taking steps towards achieving it. Good friends will be of enormous help, so be independent and self-motivated and you'll receive all the backing you need so just have courage in your convictions. Venus too lends a helping hand, ensuring that luck is on your side.

WEDNESDAY, 23RD DECEMBER
Mercury sextile Uranus

Your career plans and ambitions need to be looked at afresh. Your intuition is extremely strong at the moment, and you should follow it. There is probably no point in sticking to your original target, and it may be that the kind of job you were trained for will shortly be outdated by the advance of technology. Perhaps you need to retrain or change direction in some way.

PISCES

THURSDAY, 24TH DECEMBER
Moon square Pluto

A power struggle in your professional world is beginning to take shape and it will be a while before this is resolved. This situation may involve you directly or it may just be a case of watching without you being dragged in to it yourself. You must be careful to appear impartial and support the idea of equality for all kinds of people.

FRIDAY, 25TH DECEMBER
Moon conjunct Jupiter

Jupiter is a planet that knows no limits and that trait is passed on to you as the giant globe meets the Moon in a very sensitive area of your chart. The trouble is that though you may be exuberant and optimistic you may be too full of yourself for comfort. Try to curb any arrogant tendencies and the planetary conjunction will be beneficial. Enjoy your Christmas Day.

SATURDAY, 26TH DECEMBER
Moon square Sun

You are beginning to realize that a friend doesn't share your values. Perhaps this friend is the type who enjoys keeping you on the other end of the phone for hours on end while he or she has yet another good moan. If pointing out that your time is limited doesn't get you anywhere, you may have to give this particular pal the old heave-ho!

SUNDAY, 27TH DECEMBER
Moon square Venus

Your fondness for your friends could come under severe strain today when you realize that the cost of supplementing their enjoyment is seriously weakening your cash position. It's okay to have a good time, but you have to know when to call a halt. The bad state of your finances strikes home and you'll only have yourself to blame if you don't take a depleted bank balance seriously.

MONDAY, 28TH DECEMBER
Mercury sextile Mars

Keep your eyes and ears open and you could discover something to your advantage today. You may have to deal with some quite tricky business or financial matters, either for your employers or for yourself.

PISCES

TUESDAY, 29TH DECEMBER
Saturn direct

Your fortunes should start to improve as Saturn, that grim planet of restriction, returns to a normal course to benefit your finances. Although there could be a phase of struggling for what you want, success here is guaranteed.

WEDNESDAY, 30TH DECEMBER
Moon trine Neptune

You could be in quite an inspired mood today. This inspiration may come from within, or you could find that family members spark off a few good ideas. There is an emphasis on artistic or musical matters, so either make a start on a creative project or pop out and buy yourself a couple of new CDs to listen to.

THURSDAY, 31ST DECEMBER
Moon trine Mars

On the home front and within your closest relationships, all is harmony. Life within the family will be peaceful and pleasant and the domestic scene will be one of old-fashioned love and comfort. Happy New Year!

1999

January at a Glance

LOVE	♥		
WORK	★	★	★
MONEY	£		
HEALTH	☉	☉	☉
LUCK	♘	♘	

FRIDAY, 1ST JANUARY
Mercury square Jupiter

Don't take too much on face value today. It wouldn't be wise to base your opinions of a person on gossip because it's likely that the information you've got

PISCES

is misleading if not downright malicious. Keep an open mind and only rely on sources that are above reproach. Even then, double-check because anyone can make a mistake. Over-optimism is a factor to be watched too. Try to remain realistic on this confusing start to the New Year.

SATURDAY, 2ND JANUARY
Full Moon

Your creative soul and romantic yearnings come under the influence of today's Full Moon, so it's time to take stock of those things in your life that no longer give any emotional satisfaction. Children and younger people may need a word or two of advice now and the love lives of all around you will become the centre of interest. Your own romantic prospects may see an upturn too.

SUNDAY, 3RD JANUARY
Moon opposite Venus

Your energy level is low at the moment, so don't set yourself a list of tiresome tasks. Just go through the motions while at work. Plan an evening of resting on the sofa, watching your favourite video or chatting idly to your lover. Don't put any demands upon yourself today, get a 'take-away' dinner (a 'carry-out' to all our American readers!), and read the papers until you doze off.

MONDAY, 4TH JANUARY
Venus into Aquarius

As Venus enters your Solar house of secrets and psychology, it's obvious that the next few weeks will increase the importance of discretion in your romantic life. You'll find that it'll be wise to draw a veil over the more intimate side of your nature, and you'll be less inclined to confide your deepest secrets even to your closest friends. Quiet interludes with the one you love will be far more attractive than painting the town red just now.

TUESDAY, 5TH JANUARY
Venus conjunct Neptune

You seem to be more interested in living in a dream world than in getting to grips with reality now. You may look at a potential lover through rose-coloured glasses or you may find perfection where it doesn't exist. You need to lose touch with reality now, so indulge yourself by listening to music, going to a show, a pop concert or to any other event which will take you out of yourself and into the realms of imagination.

PISCES

WEDNESDAY, 6TH JANUARY
Moon square Pluto

There seems to be too many demands being put on you at the moment. Your partner may be keen to tell you where your duties lie, while your job or career may be demanding far too much of your time and energy. Look closely at both these situations and work out a fair and reasonable distribution of your time and effort, always remembering to leave some time for yourself too.

THURSDAY, 7TH JANUARY
Mercury into Capricorn

The swift-moving planet Mercury enters your eleventh Solar house today and gives a remarkable uplift to your social prospects. During the next few weeks you'll find yourself at the centre point of friendly interactions. People will seek you out for the pleasure of your company. It's also a good time to get in contact with distant friends and those you haven't seen for a while. The only fly in the ointment is that you shouldn't expect a small phone bill.

FRIDAY, 8TH JANUARY
Moon trine Venus

Your imagination is very powerful today, and your thoughts will turn to the romantic and erotic issues of your life again and again. It's said that dreams are quite often more fun than fact and that's certainly true of your mood today. This can't be bad for your sex life since your imagination can only provide some spice to your relationship.

SATURDAY, 9TH JANUARY
Moon square Sun

You've expended so much energy recently that it's about time you cut down on all your furious activities and took it easy for a while. Your passions are very strong at the moment with all these sudden attractions racing into your life, but it's important that you take some time to think, and to simply sit down and rest. If you don't at least try some relaxation, you'll be back to a stressed-out state in no time.

SUNDAY, 10TH JANUARY
Moon opposite Saturn

If money affairs have got you down in the dumps, take heart. The influence of the planet Saturn, though depressive can show you a way out of present difficulties. It may not be easy, and it may require a lot of thought but it is possible to improve your financial situation.

PISCES

MONDAY, 11TH JANUARY
Moon square Uranus

You feel like running away to a far-distant place, perhaps sitting in blissful peace on a romantic palm-fringed shore. Unfortunately, you can't do this today, so get to grips with reality and get those boring chores out of the way. There is nothing to stop you looking through a few holiday brochures, however, because your dreams could turn into reality at some future date.

TUESDAY, 12TH JANUARY
Venus sextile Pluto

A confidence you've kept for someone in authority should be repaid now. It always helps to have someone who is more than willing to exert a little influence on your behalf. Remember, that secrets are still there to be kept, especially when the gratitude expressed to you will point you in the direction of achieving a major ambition.

WEDNESDAY, 13TH JANUARY
Venus conjunct Uranus

You will have to keep secrets on behalf of others today. This could relate to something quite serious but it may be nothing more than helping the children buy a present for a family member. Hopefully, your personal partnerships are working well but if you are alone, it would be worth going out and about, because there is a good chance that you will meet someone interesting today.

THURSDAY, 14TH JANUARY
Sun sextile Jupiter

This is an excellent time to seek out knowledge and understanding. You may need to improve your working skills or you may simply feel like learning how to do something that will lead to an interesting hobby.

FRIDAY, 15TH JANUARY
Sun square Mars

A friend with a financial or personal problem will come to you for help. However it would not be wise to impulsively dig deep into your own resources to bail him out. Listen by all means, but more concrete help, through solving his problem would only create one of your own.

SATURDAY, 16TH JANUARY
Moon conjunct Mercury

It's a good day to get in touch with friends that you haven't seen in ages. Keep

PISCES

some blank spaces in your diary for a few select social events this week. It would be good to talk things over with some special people in your life. Though you're in a thoughtful frame of mind for much of the time it's an excellent idea to get another perspective on your plans.

SUNDAY, 17TH JANUARY
New Moon

There's no doubt that issues surrounding friendship and trust are very important now. The New Moon in your horoscopic area of social activities ensures that encounters with interesting people will yield new and enduring friendships. Though your mood has tended to vary between optimism and despair recently, the new Moon can't fail to increase your confidence and vitality.

MONDAY, 18TH JANUARY
Sun square Saturn

You are having difficulty in finalizing something which is related to your future plans. It may be that others do not share your values or priorities and they may not understand your sense of urgency. You will find it hard to relax today, so use your nervous energy in some kind of practical outlet, such as clearing out the garage or doing the garden.

TUESDAY, 19TH JANUARY
Moon conjunct Venus

You really are a soft touch today, so much so that you must avoid being taken for a ride by others. The people you help may be trying it on or in some other way trying to shift the responsibility for living their lives or paying their debts onto you. A friend may whisper secrets into your ear today and you will have to respect their confidence in you by keeping these to yourself from now on.

WEDNESDAY, 20TH JANUARY
Sun into Aquarius

The Sun moves into your house of secrets and psychology today making you very aware of your own inner world of dreams and imagination. For the next month you'll be very aware of the hurdles that face you, and all those things that tend to restrict your freedom, however your imagination and almost psychic insight will provide the necessary clues to overcome these obstacles. Issues of privacy are very important for the next few weeks.

PISCES

THURSDAY, 21ST JANUARY
Mars opposite Saturn

All mistakes have their price, and some mistakes can be very expensive indeed. Your impulses are at war with your common sense today, and men around you could be very deceptive so take extra care of your money and possessions.

FRIDAY, 22ND JANUARY
Sun conjunct Neptune

You will be called upon to help others today and you will want to give them your wholehearted support. You could need to use strange skills such as first aid or some other kind of 'rescue' skill today. Keep your wits about you because there will be strange events of one kind or another and it will be you who has to deal with them. You will be inspired in some strange way today.

SATURDAY, 23RD JANUARY
Mercury sextile Jupiter

This is an excellent day for social activities of all kinds. There's no room for negative thinking when the world seems so wonderful, and people around you are so helpful and informative. There's a lot of fun to be had in the company of good friends who supply and endless stream of gossip and chat. Mercury's combination with Jupiter makes this a pleasant, optimistic, undemanding day.

SUNDAY, 24TH JANUARY
Mercury square Saturn

It would be worth talking over your financial situation with an expert today. You may want to discuss the broad principles of your future, but your bank manager or financial adviser may be more keen to look at the details. You shouldn't get too downhearted because you are not up against insurmountable financial odds; it is just that a good sort out is needed now.

MONDAY, 25TH JANUARY
Moon square Uranus

Keep your equilibrium today if you can because the atmosphere around you will be absolute bedlam. People will be shouting at each other and nobody will be listening to anyone else. Try to keep a detached and unemotional attitude and, while you may infuriate everyone else, you will protect yourself from their madness. You may have to jump in and give practical help however.

PISCES

TUESDAY, 26TH JANUARY
Mars into Scorpio

You could find yourself travelling over great distances at some time during the next few weeks. You may be asked to visit friends or family who live overseas now or you may simply take advantage of a good holiday offer. You may restrict your travelling to mental journeys by taking up a course of study or training now.

WEDNESDAY, 27TH JANUARY
Venus sextile Saturn

Your enthusiasm about a certain person or project may be cooling just now, but that only goes to show how much you have developed as a person. A phase ends and a new one begins so look to the future with confidence.

THURSDAY, 28TH JANUARY
Venus into Pisces

The luxury-loving planet, Venus, is suggesting that this is a great time to spoil yourself and also to enjoy yourself. So treat yourself to something nice and new that is for you alone. A new outfit would be a good idea or a few nice-smelling toiletries. Throw a party for your favourite friends and don't look the other way if someone seems to be fancying you.

FRIDAY, 29TH JANUARY
Venus trine Mars

This is your chance to take your courage in both hands and make a stand for something you believe in deeply. Venus is in splendid aspect to Mars which adds just a dash of fortune to any daring action you undertake. No one will stand in your way or try to obstruct you plans. A person of the opposite sex will be very sympathetic to your ideals and aims.

SATURDAY, 30TH JANUARY
Sun sextile Pluto

Big changes are afoot in the way your career is going. However, this is nothing to be scared of. The Solar aspect to Pluto shows that you may develop a more ambitious stance and decide to improve your position or seek another post. The truly business-minded will be giving thought to striking out on your own.

SUNDAY, 31ST JANUARY
Full Moon eclipse

Changes are afoot, especially in your place of work. There may be an unexpected event to face and you may not be all that happy with the situation.

PISCES

February at a Glance

LOVE	♥	♥	♥	♥	♥
WORK	★	★	★	★	
MONEY	£	£	£	£	£
HEALTH	✚	✚	✚		
LUCK	♘				

MONDAY, 1ST FEBRUARY
Mars square Neptune

Though you may be anxious to get on, there's a nagging doubt at the back of your mind urging you against impulsive action. Do yourself a favour and listen to this cautious instinct. Otherwise you'll just be wasting time.

TUESDAY, 2ND FEBRUARY
Sun conjunct Uranus

A powerful streak of eccentricity emerges in your character today. You have a very original thought pattern now but you won't want to share any of your stunning insights just yet. The best thing you could do is to take the phone off the hook and pretend to be out and give in to the urge to be left alone to explore your ideas in peace.

WEDNESDAY, 3RD FEBRUARY
Sun conjunct Mercury

The Sun and Mercury move into close conjunction today which heightens your imagination to the point of pain. It would be too easy to get carried away with an idea now and let baseless fears rule your life. You're quite emotional now, so when the light of reason is overwhelmed by your ego, your anxieties come to the fore. Don't be taken in by flights of fancy.

THURSDAY, 4TH FEBRUARY
Moon opposite Jupiter

In the emotional stakes this is a good day but you must be careful not to over-burden your loved ones or expect too much from them. You have high expectations and those around you may feel resentful if you don't temper your

PISCES

aims with a little practicality. Rome wasn't built in a day you know so don't expect everything to go your way. There has to be some give and take.

FRIDAY, 5TH FEBRUARY
Mercury conjunct Uranus

You seem desperate to escape from reality now and it will be almost impossible for you to concentrate on the usual round of daily chores. Try to get out of the house and away from work to talk things over with a sympathetic friend because this may help you to put things into perspective or to put your mind at rest. Don't sign anything important or deal with officials today.

SATURDAY, 6TH FEBRUARY
Venus square Pluto

Venus' presence in your sign may ensure popularity with most but not with all since you're likely to be the object of envy now. The planet's aspect to Pluto hints at confrontation and heavy-handed emotional pressure today. You are a peace-loving person so someone coming on too strong will not be a welcome event. Perhaps you are being unintentionally provoking, but even so you must make the effort to avoid trouble.

SUNDAY, 7TH FEBRUARY
Moon conjunct Mars

You are in too much of a hurry to get things done today and you are likely to make mistakes as a result. More haste, less speed should be your motto today. Don't get impatient with slower people if you can help it, try channelling your zeal and zest into a constructive challenge rather than venting your spleen on those who are around you. Check the small print on any legal or official documents today.

MONDAY, 8TH FEBRUARY
Moon square Sun

There's a touch of over sensitivity about you today. We know you can usually brazen out unpleasant encounters, but just at the moment, you'd far rather completely avoid awkward situations and people. Actually this is a good thing at the moment, so don't try to force yourself into any actions that you aren't completely happy with. Being assertive could hurt your interests just now.

TUESDAY, 9TH FEBRUARY
Moon trine Jupiter

You feel the call of far-off places very keenly today. The usual round of faces and places holds no appeal as you yearn for a touch of the exotic. You need to inject

PISCES

some adventure into your life before it becomes too staid. If foreign travel is out of the question, then you should indulge yourself in anything that takes you out and about. Head for the hills ... you'll feel far better for it.

WEDNESDAY, 10TH FEBRUARY
Moon sextile Uranus

If you feel that you are being mentally boxed in, today will be the day that you find a way of breaking out of your rut. You may be bored with your job or fed up with household chores, but today you will find a way of getting over these problems and bringing some excitement into the mundane routine of your life. Let your mind roam free today and you will be rewarded with some really ingenious ideas.

THURSDAY, 11TH FEBRUARY
Mercury sextile Saturn

The financial situation may not be at its brightest, but there is a glimmer of hope today. If you can put your mind to money-making ventures, you should be able to come up with a workable scheme to enhance your earning power.

FRIDAY, 12TH FEBRUARY
Mercury into Pisces

The movement of Mercury into your own sign signals the start of a period of much clearer thinking for you. You will know where you want to go and what you want to do from now on. It will be quite easy for you to influence others with the brilliance of your ideas and you will also be able to project just the right image. Guard against trying to crowd too much into today.

SATURDAY, 13TH FEBRUARY
Jupiter into Aries

Jupiter, the giant of the zodiac moves into your Solar house of money and possessions from today, making a huge contribution to your sound judgement and generosity of spirit. You are about to acquire many material possessions, not for their own sake but for the added creature comforts that they provide. This is a planetary signal that self-indulgence is not a bad thing.

SUNDAY, 14TH FEBRUARY
Moon sextile Jupiter

You're in an extremely caring and charitable frame of mind on St Valentine's Day. Any cause that favours those who are less fortunate than you will win your wholehearted support. Not only are you ready to contribute handsomely to a fund for the needy but you'll use your influence to persuade others to do so.

PISCES

MONDAY, 15TH FEBRUARY
Moon conjunct Uranus

You seem to have an ace up your sleeve today and you may not be about to tell the world about it. If you keep things under your hat now, this will give you an edge over others in a way which wouldn't be possible if they were completely in the know. You may have a flash of inspiration today and it is even possible that you may have a peculiar flash of psychic intuition.

TUESDAY, 16TH FEBRUARY
New Moon

The eclipse shows that you are beginning to perceive a pattern in your life. All the good times, the trials and tribulations you've experienced have all had their part to play, and now you're just starting to see a grand design behind the facts of your life. I'm not promising that you'll have all the answers but at least the picture will be clearer.

WEDNESDAY, 17TH FEBRUARY
Sun sextile Saturn

Although you are concerned about money today, you must know deep down that your worries are completely unfounded. You may feel inclined to grizzle at the moment, yet the long-term projection indicates that all will eventually be well in the finances.

THURSDAY, 18TH FEBRUARY
Mercury square Pluto

The attitudes of people around you are particularly manipulative at the moment and it's important that you realize this. We know you like to help out, and will put your own desires second when it comes to the needs of someone else, but when this excellent trait is taken advantage of it's time to call a halt. Try to examine the motives of bosses and work colleagues today, for there are some underhanded goings-on that you really shouldn't deal with.

FRIDAY, 19TH FEBRUARY
Sun into Pisces

The Sun moves into your own sign today bringing with it a lifting of your spirits and a gaining of confidence in all areas of your life. Your birthday will soon be here and we hope that it will be a good one for you. You may see more of your family than is usual now and there should be some socializing and partying to look forward to. Music belongs to the realm of the Sun, so treat yourself to a musical treat very soon.

PISCES

SATURDAY, 20TH FEBRUARY
Void Moon

This is one of those days when none of the planets is making any worthwhile kind of aspect to any of the others. Even the Moon is 'void of course', which means that it is not making any aspects of any importance to any of the other planets. On such a day, avoid starting anything new and don't set out to do anything important. Do what needs to be done and take some time off for a rest.

SUNDAY, 21ST FEBRUARY
Venus into Aries

Your financial state should experience a welcome boost for a few weeks as Venus, one of the planetary indicators of wealth, moves into your Solar house of possessions and economic security from today. You feel that you deserve a lifestyle full of luxury now and that'll be reflected in the good taste you express when making purchases for your home. Your sense of self-worth is boosted too which might indicate a renewed interest in high fashion.

MONDAY, 22ND FEBRUARY
Venus sextile Neptune

You are in a kind and charitable mood today so you may decide to get involved in helping those who are handicapped in some way. Your personal values are quite spiritual at the best of times but now you will put these into action of some kind. This is a wonderful time to get involved with any kind of artistic or creative interest or to cook or make something that others can enjoy.

TUESDAY, 23RD FEBRUARY
Moon opposite Pluto

There are times when it is hard to please everyone at the same time, and today is one of those days. If you concentrate on your job, your family will grumble and if you stay at home to sort out their problems, the boss will take a dim view of you. Do something for everyone while, in the meantime looking for ways in which you can avoid this situation occurring again.

WEDNESDAY, 24TH FEBRUARY
Venus conjunct Jupiter

As far as money goes, today's conjunction between Jupiter and Venus heralds a time when you can't go wrong. Both Venus and Jupiter are beneficial planets and they bring abundant star luck to bear on all personal finances and possessions. Make the most of this wonderful period of opportunity because you can boost both your income and your feelings of self-worth at the same time.

PISCES

THURSDAY, 25TH FEBRUARY
Moon trine Sun

You're in the mood to enjoy life to the absolute full today. The Moon splendidly aspects the Sun which enables you to find humour in the most ordinary circumstances. You should get the chance to indulge yourself in a favourite hobby. The more creative the better. For those of a romantic turn of mind, today should present the opportunity for a wonderful amorous liaison.

FRIDAY, 26TH FEBRUARY
Sun trine Mars

An action-packed and fortunate day as the Sun contacts Mars. A good time to travel in company, and men in your life will be attentive and flattering. Intellectual pursuits too will go very well.

SATURDAY, 27TH FEBRUARY
Jupiter sextile Neptune

This is a great day to dream up money-making ideas…no matter how far-fetched they may seem! The planet Neptune provides the inspiration while Jupiter brings you all the luck you'll need to make your schemes work!

SUNDAY, 28TH FEBRUARY
Moon opposite Uranus

You may be felled by some kind of sudden and unexpected infection today or you may be recovering from a recent injury or accident. Either way, you are not at your best and should, therefore, avoid doing anything too strenuous. You may get into trouble by doing something with the very best of intentions, only to find that this is misconstrued or thrown back in your face. Nervous tension proliferates today, so try to relax.

PISCES

March at a Glance

LOVE	♥	♥			
WORK	★	★	★		
MONEY	£	£	£	£	
HEALTH	✪	✪	✪		
LUCK	♄	♄	♄	♄	♄

MONDAY, 1ST MARCH
Saturn into Taurus

Saturn moves into the communications sector of your horoscope from today for a stay of some years. This period should see a deepening of your thoughts, a more considered attitude and, possibly, a desire to remedy shortcomings in your past education. Travel in connection with solid aims, either in business or family affairs is favoured.

TUESDAY, 2ND MARCH
Mercury into Aries

All the planets seem to be restless just now since Mercury changes sign today. At least you can get your mind into gear concerning the state of your finances now. Tasks you've been putting off like cancelling useless standing orders, or ensuring you receive the most advantageous interest from your savings will be tackled with ease now.

WEDNESDAY, 3RD MARCH
Venus trine Pluto

There could be some kind of subtle power game going on around you at the moment and a bit of consideration may show you just who and what is trying to pull your strings. If you are invited to some kind of formal gathering, it would be well worth putting in an appearance if only to ensure that no decisions are taken behind your back. You may be inspired by something musical or artistic today.

THURSDAY, 4TH MARCH
Venus sextile Uranus

Where money is concerned, planning goes out the window today. However, this

PISCES

is not bad news. Venus the indicator of cash luck is in good aspect to the planet of surprises so a windfall from an unexpected source is likely for many.

FRIDAY, 5TH MARCH
Mercury sextile Neptune

Something will inspire you today and it may set your imagination alight. This 'something' may be a song or a piece of music or it may be something that you read or that you see on the television. A friend may make a suggestion that sets you on the road to some kind of creative success. The rather mystical feeling which comes from today's planets can also make you vulnerable to thieves and cheats, so take care!

SATURDAY, 6TH MARCH
Moon square Neptune

It's not really a day to get your head around anything, certainly not anything important. You may feel that you have tied up loose ends but everything, especially travel arrangements should be double-checked. Leave nothing to chance for warning bells are sounding within your unconscious mind.

SUNDAY, 7TH MARCH
Moon square Uranus

You are in a strangely rebellious mood today and, perhaps in some strange way, this is a good thing. You may have been putting up with some things that don't suit you for far too long and now is the time to make others aware that this is not going to continue. Try not to allow your temper to get out of hand in case you say something that you regret or in case you shut the door to reconciliation for good.

MONDAY, 8TH MARCH
Moon trine Venus

Attend to practical matters today and deal with anything to do with money now. If you talk to your bank manager about finances for a business idea, you will get some really useful advice and most probably all the help you require to go along with this. If you need to save up for some kind of future event or a future project, then set this in motion soon.

TUESDAY, 9TH MARCH
Moon trine Jupiter

You have every reason in the world to be confident and outgoing today. The Moon's aspect to Jupiter makes you one of the most optimistic and popular

PISCES

people around. Financially, good news is on its way. We're not promising anything spectacular but you'll still be smiling. If you want to take full advantage of today's stars then work out an investment plan with someone who knows the best policy.

WEDNESDAY, 10TH MARCH
Mercury retrograde

It's typical, just as Mercury was getting to grips with your financial state, the wayward planet backtracks sending all cash affairs into chaos once more. At least this is a temporary problem. However, you'll have to take extra trouble to be completely clear in financial matters. Check all facts and figure thoroughly just to be on the safe side.

THURSDAY, 11TH MARCH
Moon square Mercury

A friend may tell you something that upsets you today while another friend may do something that costs you money. With friends like these, do you really need enemies? Your mind is not working at its best now so don't agree to anything or do anything that you are unhappy about or unsure about. Wait until your judgement is working at full strength once again.

FRIDAY, 12TH MARCH
Moon sextile Mars

It's a time for you to show off your social skills. Friends, old and new are out there waiting for you. I'll bet you didn't know you were so popular. Go to any gathering and you'll be the centre of attention. You could hear from an old friend who is overseas at the moment.

SATURDAY, 13TH MARCH
Mercury sextile Neptune

Ever since Neptune entered your area of deep psychology you will have been prone to meaningful dreams and psychic experiences. Now you can turn some of these inspirations into fact. Follow your hunches now, and you'll find that they lead to profit.

SUNDAY, 14TH MARCH
Moon sextile Pluto

Give some thought to your position in life now because you may realize that you are on the wrong path, or that you are being diverted from the right pathway now. You may only need to make a few adjustments in order to bring your life and your ambitions back into line again. You will get more co-operation from

PISCES

others by being kind and thoughtful than by trying to manipulate them, but do both if you want to be absolutely sure of success!

MONDAY, 15TH MARCH
Moon sextile Venus

If you can possibly manage to get away from the rat race today it would be a marvellous idea. The Lunar aspect to Venus shows that your mind isn't on worldly duties at all now so you may as well relax that fevered brow and try to renew your energies by taking it easy. It doesn't matter what you do to pass the time as long as you enjoy yourself. Perhaps you should indulge in a little luxury, the treat would do you good.

TUESDAY, 16TH MARCH
Moon square Pluto

Keep your eye on any power games that are going on in your place of work. If somebody suggests some kind of rearrangement of the current seating plan or work space allocation, then make sure that you are not sidelined into a cold and inhospitable corner. If you have to fight for your rights, do so with a little tact because everyone knows that you can catch more flies with honey than with vinegar. (Who wants to catch flies anyway?)

WEDNESDAY, 17TH MARCH
New Moon

There's a New Moon in your own sign. This is a powerfully positive influence that encourages you to make a new start. Personal opportunities are about to change your life. You must now be prepared to leave the past behind to embark on a brand new course. Decide what you want, because you'll be your own best guide now.

THURSDAY, 18TH MARCH
Venus into Taurus

If you've got any favours to ask, the passage of Venus into your Solar house of persuasion shows that you can use considerable charm and eloquence to win others over to your point of view with little trouble at all. A little flirtation combined with a winning way ensures that you achieve your desires. Your creative talents are boosted too so perhaps you should consider writing down your inspirations now.

FRIDAY, 19TH MARCH
Sun conjunct Mercury

Mercury and the Sun are in conjunction in your own sign today. This will bring

PISCES

success on many different fronts for you. Mercury is especially effective in regard to any form of communication. Therefore, if you need to get on the phone and to deal with things, you will make excellent progress today. It is a good day for starting projects, finding work or writing of any kind, so get going on that novel you have been thinking of for so long!

SATURDAY, 20TH MARCH
Venus conjunct Saturn

It's a day of very mixed planetary influences when Venus meets Saturn. You could learn something very deep and meaningful in a casual or even frivolous setting. Be aware of undercurrents in the jokes and apparently idle comments of friends. A message will be passed to you, but are you subtle enough to pick up on the full meaning? If you're at all educationally minded, you may consider pursuing an old interest that was abandoned through no fault of your own.

SUNDAY, 21ST MARCH
Sun into Aries

Your financial prospects take an upturn from today as the Sun enters your house of money and possessions. The next month should see an improvement in your economic security. It may be that you need to lay plans to ensure maximum profit now. Don't expect any swift returns for investments but lay down a pattern for future growth. Sensible monetary decisions made now will pay off in a big way.

MONDAY, 22ND MARCH
Moon trine Neptune

The whole idea of getting in touch with your emotions can make you a trifle uncomfortable but why stand on the outside looking in when there is a real chance to feel love? Try taking a risk and revealing your sensitive side and you will be surprised at the wonderful reception that others will give you. Married or settled readers will find their domestic surroundings strangely inspiring today.

TUESDAY, 23RD MARCH
Venus square Neptune

You are likely to hear some strange and confusing items of news today because a woman relative or friend may have some really odd news to pass on. Don't act on this until you have checked it out and, even then, only do something if you absolutely must. There are some hard facts to be faced if one particular ambition of yours is to succeed.

PISCES

WEDNESDAY, 24TH MARCH
Moon square Sun

The quest for happiness can sometimes be more expensive than you expect. All you want to do is have some fun, but how far are you prepared to go to find it? It could be that you are trying to escape from an unpleasant fact of life by drowning your sorrows.

THURSDAY, 25TH MARCH
Sun sextile Neptune

There seem to be emotional undercurrents going on around you that need a bit of attention. You will have just the kind of words which would resolve the situation right on the tip of your tongue today. In addition to this, you will be able to put quite difficult situations right without giving offence. You will be drawn to help others now, perhaps by helping out at a local charity event.

FRIDAY, 26TH MARCH
Moon square Saturn

A small health worry could easily bring you down today. The Moon's aspect to Saturn will make you prone to hypochondria. The most minor symptom will be blown out of all proportion. The cause of this may be a work worry that is playing on your mind. Try to be more positive about it. Fretting over a situation you can't change will only make you feel worse.

SATURDAY, 27TH MARCH
Venus opposite Mars

It's not a great day for neighbourhood harmony since the most minor mishap will be blown up into a good approximation of World War III! You can't even easily escape because travel too is a dodgy area when Venus opposes Mars.

SUNDAY, 28TH MARCH
Void Moon

Occasionally one finds a day in which neither the planets nor the Moon make any major aspects to each other and on such a day, the Moon's course is said to be 'void'. There is nothing wrong with a day like this but there is no point in trying to start anything new or anything important because there isn't enough of a planetary boost to get it off the ground. Stick to your normal routine.

MONDAY, 29TH MARCH
Moon square Pluto

It may be a difficult day to deal with bosses or your partner. You have to remember that those around you have worries too so don't be too offended if they seem cool and distant now.

TUESDAY, 30TH MARCH

Jupiter trine Pluto

The aspect between Jupiter and Pluto indicates a lucky break in connection with your career. Even if you haven't previously been at all ambitious, you should now feel the urge to go right to the top! This is a go-getting force which will push you onward and upward!

WEDNESDAY, 31ST MARCH

Full Moon

The Full Moon brings to the surface intense feelings that you have buried away in some vault of memory. You'll be forced to look at yourself stripped bare of illusions now. That's not such a bad things because you'll realize that many of your hang-ups have been a total waste of time and should be ditched. You may have a financial worry coming to a head so today's Full Moon encourages you to take decisive action to sort it out once and for all.

April at a Glance

LOVE	♥	♥	♥		
WORK	★	★	★	★	★
MONEY	£	£	£		
HEALTH	✚	✚	✚	✚	
LUCK	∪	∪	∪		

THURSDAY, 1ST APRIL

Sun conjunct Jupiter

Opportunity knocks today! The Sun unites with Jupiter in your house of finances and releases all the generosity inherent in the huge planet. Money luck is certain with such a powerful planetary duo. Cash comes to your hand more easily than it has recently, however you will tend to spend it too! But, even the most spendthrift couldn't fail to gain on a day when pennies seem to rain from heaven.

PISCES

FRIDAY, 2ND APRIL
Mercury direct

At last, Mercury turns tail and starts to move forward, bringing to an end a period of confusion or mental frustration that has had you in its grip for the last two or three weeks. You can embark on serious negotiations with others now if needs be and you can move ahead with all kinds of business matters. Any trips which have been delayed can now be taken and muddles and mishaps will soon be cleared up.

SATURDAY, 3RD APRIL
Moon conjunct Mars

You're quite impatient and assertive today which points to a strong Lunar aspect to Mars. It's a particularly restless time for you. You don't want to spend any time explaining your actions or viewpoints so woe betide anyone who dares to hold you up. This aggressive you isn't going to get you anywhere though so do try to slow down and think things through before you fly off the handle.

SUNDAY, 4TH APRIL
Mercury sextile Venus

You'll be extremely lucid and charming today. If you have any favours to ask, then ask them now because very few could respond negatively to your reasoned arguments and winning smile. This is a good day to travel and to show your personality off to its best advantage.

MONDAY, 5TH APRIL
Moon sextile Neptune

Though there are certain problems relating to your career at the moment, it isn't wise to over-react. Think things through once more. A few moments spent by yourself will clarify recent hectic events.

TUESDAY, 6TH APRIL
Saturn square Neptune

When the mind overheats, there's very little to stop irrational fears and suspicions surfacing. Your neighbourhood is the arena for this unwarranted disquiet and you could find yourself at odds over nothing at all. Keep your opinions to yourself if you want to avoid trouble!

WEDNESDAY, 7TH APRIL
Sun sextile Uranus

You have a golden opportunity to make somebody's dreams come true today and

PISCES

perhaps that somebody is yourself. If there is something you really fancy doing, then take a chance and make a start on this now because the outlook for success is really quite good. You have a strong impulse to help others now and, while this is all very admirable, try not to wear yourself out doing it.

THURSDAY, 8TH APRIL
Moon sextile Mars

A friend who has been aware of your dissatisfaction and boredom will show the way forward to a more fulfilling way of life. If you feel stuck in a rut, then follow the lead of your adventurous companion. You won't regret falling in with any travel plans which will expand your experience. Don't be afraid to go beyond the limits of normal habits now.

FRIDAY, 9TH APRIL
Moon sextile Mercury

Prepare yourself for a party. It may not be planned but the Lunar aspect to Mercury ensures that an impromptu affair has all the makings of a splendid time. Forget your duties for now, and accept any invitation that comes your way without a second thought. On the other hand you may find your home invaded by friends determined on a good time.

SATURDAY, 10TH APRIL
Moon square Saturn

I'm afraid that there's a fairly depressing influence about the Lunar aspect to Saturn today. It won't take much effort to think about all the things that possibly could go wrong in your life. The old enemy pessimism is back with a vengeance. Perhaps the cause of your worry is an elderly neighbour, or even closer, a brother or sister who is having considerable problems. Try to be calm and look on the bright side.

SUNDAY, 11TH APRIL
Moon sextile Sun

Money may be the root of all evil but it's worse still not having any! It is obvious that you are doing a lot of thinking about the state of your finances, and more importantly, the things of true value in your life today.

MONDAY, 12TH APRIL
Venus into Gemini

Old scores and family squabbles can now be laid to rest as the passage of Venus into your domestic area signals a time of harmony and contentment. Surround

PISCES

yourself with beauty, both in terms of affection and in material possessions. This is a good time to renew a closeness with those you love. Join forces to complete a major project such as redecoration, or even a move of home itself. Be assured that the stars smile on you now.

TUESDAY, 13TH APRIL
Moon sextile Venus

Anyone who wishes to provoke you by starting on a controversial subject will be surprised when you retreat in panic. Serious topics are the last thing you want to tackle today. In fact, you'd far rather a conversation based on more mundane matters. You need a good laugh so some wit and gossip would be appreciated. Steer clear of anything too heavy.

WEDNESDAY, 14TH APRIL
Moon into Aries

Today's Lunar positions puts a worrying spotlight on the state of your finances. You could spend some time working out a sensible budget or going through your accounts to sort out the wheat from the chaff. Unnecessary expenses should be curtailed now. A pragmatic financial view will save you a lot of embarrassment later.

THURSDAY, 15TH APRIL
Moon conjunct Jupiter

This could be a red-letter day as far as financial matters are concerned. You could also be gratified to learn that other people share your outlook and that they also understand your objectives in life. You may want to form a partnership for some reason now and this too is well starred today.

FRIDAY, 16TH APRIL
New Moon

Today's New Moon shows that your financial affairs have reached a point where you have to make a decision. Do you carry on in the old, and rather dreary ways of making and spending your cash or will you look at the realities and make sensible decisions? This isn't a time to retreat into dreamland, or to carry on with bad budgeting. Look at your monetary state carefully now.

SATURDAY, 17TH APRIL
Mercury into Aries

Mercury's timely entry into your financial sector should be a great help to your situation. Your mind will now be clear and you can see all issues from a logical

PISCES

standpoint. Now you'll be able to budget sensibly, pay off outstanding debts and generally make sense of your cash flow. The shrewdness that Mercury brings to bear on your economic life will enable you to control income and expenditure.

SUNDAY, 18TH APRIL
Moon conjunct Venus

This should be a good day for your family and your home life. Relatives may pop in with offers of help and useful gifts. Any family gathering that happens now will be extremely successful. This is a good time to buy something beautiful or valuable for your home or to arrange for refurbishment to be done to it. This is a good day to pick up collectors' items such as antiques or *objets d'art*.

MONDAY, 19TH APRIL
Mars opposite Saturn

It's not going to be an easy day if you want anything done in a hurry! Mars opposes Saturn showing that your impatience is at fever pitch but that the circumstances are such that you'll have to slow down rather than speed up. If travelling, expect hitches and delays.

TUESDAY, 20TH APRIL
Sun into Taurus

Your curiosity will be massively stimulated from today as the Sun enters your area of learning and communication. Other people's business suddenly becomes your own now, since many will turn to you for advice and guidance. Affairs in the lives of your brothers, sisters and neighbours have extra importance now. Short journeys too are well starred for one month.

WEDNESDAY, 21ST APRIL
Venus opposite Pluto

Your feelings are particularly intense today and you will be ready to leap to the defence of colleagues and family members on the slightest pretext. Getting worked up over domestic or work issues will only send your blood pressure soaring so try to keep calm.

THURSDAY, 22ND APRIL
Mercury sextile Neptune

Hunches should be followed now! Your intuition is on form and your perceptions will be pretty psychic. Before you dismiss this as wishful thinking, mull it over. You'll find that your deep unconscious mind is trying to tell you something.

PISCES

FRIDAY, 23RD APRIL
Jupiter sextile Uranus

A fortunate turn of events will come now after a period of unexpected losses. This is a true change in your fortunes and all worries will soon be eased. Money concerns especially are set for rapid improvement!

SATURDAY, 24TH APRIL
Sun opposite Mars

The Sun opposes Mars today so outbursts of temper are quite likely especially when you are confronted with daft opinions, entrenched prejudices and downright stupidity. You won't tolerate fools now and see no reason why people can't see past their own ignorance. If the company of fools irritates you so much you should absent yourself completely because any over-reaction from you is likely to rebound in totally unpredictable ways.

SUNDAY, 25TH APRIL
Moon trine Saturn

There's no doubt that you've been too busy to let your other half in on everything you're doing but you do get the chance to alleviate all suspicions by coming out into the open today. Perhaps you haven't wanted to share you anxieties with your partner up to now, but it's important to remember that a problem shared is a problem halved.

MONDAY, 26TH APRIL
Mercury trine Pluto

Talks behind closed doors will work in your favour today. You may be discussed by employers and other authority figures who reckon that you deserve more scope to show off your talents. If you are attending interviews you can be sure of saying the right things and giving the right impression.

TUESDAY, 27TH APRIL
Sun conjunct Saturn

This should be a sober and practical day in most ways. The Sun meets up with Saturn now which brings out the most pragmatic and serious side to your nature. Frivolous comments and idle jokes will find no favour with you now because you're far too wrapped up in serious issues to be bothered with flighty people. Your thoughts will be deep and profound so a conversation on serious topics with someone like-minded should be your favourite activity of the day.

PISCES

WEDNESDAY, 28TH APRIL
Moon opposite Mercury

You're full of bright and stunning ideas today and we just hope some of them take romantic interest into account because you could cause some serious offence if they don't! Serious offence is a bit of a theme since your capacity for tact is at an all-time low. Face it, you can be too truthful for comfort sometimes and today's Lunar opposition to Mercury could put other's backs up simply because you are too candid. Remember to write down your ideas because they're so good you shouldn't waste any of them.

THURSDAY, 29TH APRIL
Mercury sextile Uranus

Inventive ways of making, or saving money is your forte today. If anyone could spot a bargain it's you! Even a quick trip down to the shops could yield some surprises, and you may return loaded with the bags of things that were so cheap you just had to buy, rather than the simple loaf of bread that you'd gone out for in the first place.

FRIDAY, 30TH APRIL
Full Moon

You may have to face the fact that you cannot slope off to distant and romantic shores just now. This doesn't mean that you are forever confined to your home, just that you cannot get away right now. Your mood is not only escapist but also rebellious today! You won't want to have anything to do with people who restrict you or who remind you of your chores and duties but you simply won't be able to escape them.

May at a Glance

LOVE	♥	♥	♥	♥	♥
WORK	★	★	★		
MONEY	£	£	£	£	
HEALTH	✪	✪			
LUCK	♘	♘	♘		

PISCES

SATURDAY, 1ST MAY
Mercury conjunct Jupiter

Mercury's conjunction with Jupiter is bound to bring some good news concerning your cash flow. It may be only a promise at the moment, yet there's every possibility that you're in for a windfall. Luck is on your side now, but don't rely on it too much as you could blow all your gains before you actually receive them! Be sensible and your monetary good fortune will be secure.

SUNDAY, 2ND MAY
Moon sextile Neptune

This is a day for laying plans and working out subtle strategies. Don't allow yourself to be pressured into making sudden moves in any area, but most especially in the workplace. Think carefully before you act.

MONDAY, 3RD MAY
Moon sextile Uranus

You should have a lucky break in connection with your job now. If you don't work, or if work is not your first priority, then something good will occur which helps you to reach your personal goals. It may be that something comes to light which was hidden from view up to now. For example, if you have lost or mislaid something, it could now emerge from its hiding place.

TUESDAY, 4TH MAY
Moon opposite Venus

Your life needs some kind of alteration or rearranging now. You may have too many burdens being placed upon you at the moment both at home and at work and you will need to sort these out soon before they break your back in two. You may need more help from those around you or you may have to take on some kind of staff to do some of your jobs for you.

WEDNESDAY, 5TH MAY
Mars into Libra

Mars moves into your Solar eighth house today, raising the level of your feelings to some kind of fever pitch. Your passions will be aroused in some important way and you could find yourself behaving in an unusual manner due to the depth of your emotions. Make sure that you are not simply reacting out of anger or out of some kind of feverish response to anything today.

PISCES

THURSDAY, 6TH MAY
Moon square Jupiter

Don't be too ready to believe all you hear today. It's too likely that you'll be led up the garden path by an acquaintance who is out to deceive you for his or her own gain. Be suspicious of high-flown promises and words that paint scenarios that are too good to be true. One last word of warning …. Don't part with any cash, or you'll find that it's the last you'll see of it.

FRIDAY, 7TH MAY
Neptune retrograde

Something will force you to question your spiritual certainties now and this will gradually lead you to a newer and wider manner of thinking in the future. You must guard against getting involved with any kind of self-destructive behaviour because this may be very hard to overcome once it becomes ingrained. Look carefully into your unconscious motivations now.

SATURDAY, 8TH MAY
Mercury into Taurus

Your mind will be going at full speed ahead over the next few weeks and you are bound to come up with some really great new ideas. You will be very busy with the phone ringing off its hook and letters falling into your letter box by the ton. You will find yourself acting as a temporary secretary for a while, even if the only person who makes use of your services is yourself.

SUNDAY, 9TH MAY
Mercury sextile Venus

You could fall madly, deeply and truly in love today! In fact, if you so much as step outside your own front door, you will be sure to attract at least one interesting member of the opposite sex. If you are already in a happy relationship, then the feelings between you and your lover will deepen and deepen under this planetary aspect.

MONDAY, 10TH MAY
Moon square Pluto

A power struggle in your professional world is beginning to take shape and it will be a while before this is resolved. This situation may involve you directly or it may just be a case of watching this played out in front of you without you being dragged into it yourself. You must be careful to appear impartial and also to support the idea of equality for all kinds of people.

PISCES

TUESDAY, 11TH MAY
Mercury square Neptune

Don't take on too much today! Your mind will feel as if it's full of cotton wool and anything you say will be misunderstood. Keep yourself to yourself if you want to avoid confusion.

WEDNESDAY, 12TH MAY
Moon trine Pluto

There is bright news as far as money and work are concerned now. Circumstances are changing around you and there will be a definite spin-off of benefits coming in your direction. You may have to wait for others to make their moves before you can do much. However, you must also be aware of the need for flexibility because it may be that you need to make a fundamental change in your attitude or usual work practices in order to succeed.

THURSDAY, 13TH MAY
Mercury conjunct Saturn

You're likely to be in very serious frame of mind today as Mercury, planet of thought meets up with Saturn, ruler of patient effort. Now, you'll want to explore underlying problems and provide solutions. Deep conversations and meaningful thoughts are the order of the day.

FRIDAY, 14TH MAY
Moon sextile Venus

Younger members of the family will surprise you by welcoming you home with a meal cooked and the house all cleared up. Don't forget to thank them profusely and to show real appreciation of their efforts. A woman may be helpful in connection with a project that you are working on at the moment.

SATURDAY, 15TH MAY
New Moon

The New Moon shows a change in your way of thinking. In many ways you'll know that it's time to move on. Perhaps you'll find yourself in a new company, a new home or among a new circle of friends in the near future. Opinions are set to change as you are influenced by more stimulating people. Perhaps you'll consider taking up an educational course of some kind.

SUNDAY, 16TH MAY
Venus sextile Saturn

If someone you love is troubled you'll have to take special care to show your trust

PISCES

and loyalty today. Venus is aspected to Saturn which promotes a need for you to show your faith, and that you are a pillar of support to the one that needs you most. Ignore negative moods and coldness and look beyond the obvious to the root cause of the problem.

MONDAY, 17TH MAY
Mercury square Uranus

Many of your inventive ideas are very good indeed, but you'll find that today you aren't at your most lucid. If you try to explain anything, you'll find your audience more confused than they were in the first place.

TUESDAY, 18TH MAY
Moon sextile Saturn

The path of true love doesn't always run smoothly as we all know, but you can restore harmony by being open about your feelings especially your anxieties today. You'll meet with comfort and support from a loved one.

WEDNESDAY, 19TH MAY
Moon square Jupiter

If you're a gambling sort, you'll be strongly tempted to part with some cash on what seems to be a sure winner today. Unfortunately, the Moon and Jupiter conspire to make your confidence misplaced. Any money laid out on pleasure is gone forever. This applies to any leisure activity now. If you can afford the outlay, there's no problem. If not, then don't risk it because there's no windfall due today.

THURSDAY, 20TH MAY
Moon opposite Neptune

You may be under par today and you may not know exactly what it is that ails you. There could be a psychological reason for your current feelings of malaise while for women there could be a temporary hormonal imbalance. Your job may be getting you down at the moment and, even if there is nothing obviously wrong at your workplace, you may feel that something is not as it should be.

FRIDAY, 21ST MAY
Sun into Gemini

The home and family become your main interest over the next four weeks as the Sun moves into the most domestic area of your chart from today. Family feuds will now be resolved, and you'll find an increasing contentment in your own surroundings. A haven of peace will be restored in your home. This should also be a period of nostalgia when happy memories come flooding back.

PISCES

SATURDAY, 22ND MAY
Uranus retrograde

Over the next few weeks you will be aware of a slight slowing down in your affairs. You may have to take things easy because of a health matter or you may just be aware that all your plans will have to be put on the back burner for a while. Circumstances may suddenly change around you, causing you a good deal of mental confusion and, even if outside events don't hold you up, you may simply decide to let things rest for a while.

SUNDAY, 23RD MAY
Mercury into Gemini

The past exerts a powerful influence as Mercury enters the house of heritage. You'll find that things long forgotten will somehow re-enter your life over the next couple of weeks. An interest in your family heritage may develop, or possibly a new-found passion for antiques. Some good, meaningful conversations in the family will prove enlightening.

MONDAY, 24TH MAY
Moon trine Mercury

There is a highly charged atmosphere around you just now and this is forcing you to look at your home situation and also your joint financial arrangements. Today's excellent aspects between the Moon and Mercury suggest that you will be able to talk over some of your worries with those you are close to. It may be a good idea to chat about joint financial matters while you are about it too.

TUESDAY, 25TH MAY
Sun trine Neptune

The work you have been putting in on your home, garden or any land that you own is beginning to pay off now; at least it looks very good now. The same is true for those of you who work from home or who run small businesses. You should get in touch with your family now and give them the support and understanding that they need.

WEDNESDAY, 26TH MAY
Sun conjunct Mercury

A good chat with a relative could open up possibilities and reveal old secrets today. The Sun meets up with Mercury in your Solar house of heritage and family issues so you'll take a great deal of pleasure in the company of those who are close to you. This should also be a time to look to the future. Perhaps a move of home should be considered now.

PISCES

THURSDAY, 27TH MAY
Moon square Neptune

You are rather dissatisfied today. Nothing that is familiar will hold any appeal at all. What you need is a change. If you can find this by travel so much the better. However, you can achieve the same effect by opening up your mind. Read a good book as it educates as well as entertains.

FRIDAY, 28TH MAY
Moon square Uranus

Privacy is something that you'd give your eye-teeth for at the moment, unfortunately there's very little on offer. You need some time alone to formulate your thoughts but unexpected events will interrupt you again and again. Anything from a constantly ringing phone, to someone who calls in on the off chance is a possibility. Try to retain your composure; after all you can always pretend to be out or take the phone off the hook.

SATURDAY, 29TH MAY
Mars opposite Jupiter

A man seems to be making a point of behaving in an awkward and obstructive manner towards you today. You and a partner or close associate may disagree over the way you spend your money now.

SUNDAY, 30TH MAY
Full Moon

Today's Full Moon shows that important decisions have to be made at a time of rapidly changing circumstances. News that arrives today could well be disturbing yet will prove to be a blessing in disguise in the long run. You may be considering a move of home, possibly to a distant location. Or even throwing in your present career to take up an educational course of some kind. People you meet while travelling will have important words to say.

MONDAY, 31ST MAY
Venus square Mars

There seems to be some kind of hitch in your love life at the moment and it is hard for you to get the kind of togetherness with your loved one that you want. Some of you may decide now that your current partnership is no longer viable and thus start to make plans for a solo existence in the future. If there is an unwanted suitor hanging around you now, you will finally find a way to tell him or her that you don't want them near you any more.

PISCES

June at a Glance

LOVE	♥				
WORK	★	★	★	★	★
MONEY	£				
HEALTH	✪	✪	✪	✪	
LUCK	♄	♄	♄	♄	

TUESDAY, 1ST JUNE
Venus square Jupiter

Shopping sprees should be a definite no-no today. Your self-control is at its weakest under the negative influence of Venus and Jupiter. Temptation crosses your path again and again now, so put away the cheque book and credit cards for the stars show you to be in a spendthrift mood, capable of purchasing any old rubbish just for the sake of it. You'll regret the squandering of your resources tomorrow.

WEDNESDAY, 2ND JUNE
Sun opposite Pluto

You may look quite calm on the outside but, like a volcano, there is a good deal boiling away under the surface and it looks likely to erupt fairly soon. You may need some extra help, either in the home or at your place of work because you are finding it increasingly difficult to keep all your plates in the air at the same time.

THURSDAY, 3RD JUNE
Mars direct

Personal problems that have been an underlying issue in your life since January will take a step nearer to resolution from today. Mars again turns into his proper course enabling you to talk over many private issues that have caused embarrassment and hang-ups. Joint financial ventures should receive fresh impetus at this time.

PISCES

FRIDAY, 4TH JUNE
Mercury trine Mars

If you've been tied in a knot about a legal or financial matter you'll be amazed how quickly the clouds disperse when a family member sees through the complications to the underlying issues. Don't be afraid to listen to a new point of view. You'll be amazed how quickly you take it on board and how easy it is to deal with the most confusing situation. Two heads are better than one today.

SATURDAY, 5TH JUNE
Venus into Leo

Venus moves out of the fun, sun and pleasure area of your chart into the work, duty and health area, and it will stay there for the next few weeks. This suggests that any problems related to work and duty will become easier to handle and also that you could start to see some kind of practical outcome from all that you have been doing lately. If you have been off-colour recently, Venus will help you to feel better soon.

SUNDAY, 6TH JUNE
Moon square Pluto

You may feel that you are being pushed or manipulated into a position which doesn't suit you. You know your own worth and you are not about to have it minimized by others, therefore if you feel that you are not being treated fairly and squarely by those who are around you, you are liable to lose your temper with them today. Pour out your troubles to an understanding friend.

MONDAY, 7TH JUNE
Mercury into Cancer

Mercury moves into a part of your horoscope that is concerned with creativity. Mercury rules such things as thinking, learning and communications, but it can also be associated with skills and craftwork of various kinds. The combination of creativity and craftwork suggests that the next few weeks would be a good time to work on hobbies such as dressmaking, carpentry and so on.

TUESDAY, 8TH JUNE
Sun trine Uranus

Even though your personal taste might incline to some solitude it's very unlikely that you'll get the luxury of following your desire today. Unexpected visitors are due, so put the kettle on.

PISCES

WEDNESDAY, 9TH JUNE
Moon sextile Uranus

You may get some kind of bright money-making idea today, although a simple examination of your financial position may be all that is needed to keep you on the right track now. Something odd will make you examine your values and priorities today and it will become clear that you need to keep to the straight and narrow and to avoid doing anything which could be harmful to yourself or to others.

THURSDAY, 10TH JUNE
Venus opposite Neptune

Women are likely to screw you up completely today. You will hear so many conflicting things from them that you won't know whether you are coming or going. Guard against getting sucked into a problem which is not of your making and which you cannot really put right. For example, if you have a friend who drinks or who is on drugs, don't try to cure him or her, you won't be able to do it and you will have your heart broken in the meantime.

FRIDAY, 11TH JUNE
Moon square Uranus

Try not to let your habit of coming out with risqué or shocking statements get the better of you today. However, if you must vent a bit of steam or have a bit of fun at someone else's expense, do so among friends who understand the ground rules rather than at work or in an inappropriate social situation. There is a fine line between being outspoken and being objectionable and you could be skating very close to it today.

SATURDAY, 12TH JUNE
Moon trine Neptune

You could be in quite an inspired mood today. This inspiration may come from inside your own head or you could find that family members spark off a few good ideas. There is an emphasis on artistic or musical matters today, so either make a start on some kind of artistic project or pop out and buy yourself a couple of interesting new CDs to listen to.

SUNDAY, 13TH JUNE
New Moon

The New Moon falls in the sphere of home and family today indicating a need for a change. For some reason you've been dissatisfied with your domestic set-up so you may consider looking at house prices in your own or indeed another area.

PISCES

You probably feel that you need more space and light in your life that your present home isn't providing. A family member may be considering setting up home and deserves all the encouragement you can give.

MONDAY, 14TH JUNE
Venus trine Pluto

Feelings run deep today, and you'll get the distinct impression that there's something going on behind the scenes at work. Maybe your partner isn't telling you what's on his or her mind. There is no cause for alarm. Whatever the outcome of these secret dealing, they're unlikely to be to your disadvantage.

TUESDAY, 15TH JUNE
Mercury sextile Saturn

A serious attitude will win you far more respect than any witty remarks. You need to show your lover the inner you and that you have deep thoughts. You'll encounter understanding and agreement with your views.

WEDNESDAY, 16TH JUNE
Sun trine Mars

The strong aspect between the Sun and Mars turns you into a tornado around the home. You've got enormous reserves of energy now so you'll be inclined to tackle a thousand and one little jobs around the home. Neglected chores should prove no problem whatsoever. On a more personal note, the passionate side of your nature should find some physical expression too.

THURSDAY, 17TH JUNE
Moon opposite Uranus

A sudden and unexpected happening in your place of work could serve to give you doubts about whether you are doing the right kind of job or if there is enough room for advancement in your line of work. If you wake up feeling under par, then rest, relax and maybe try an unorthodox kind of treatment because it seems that you are more likely to respond to something like reflexology or aromatherapy just now.

FRIDAY, 18TH JUNE
Moon trine Jupiter

Today's stars give you the chance to prove that there's not a mean or petty bone in your body... well, not at the moment anyway! The combination of the Moon and Jupiter enables you to forgive most misdemeanours today. You're also an extremely dependable sort of person whom other's can rely on.

PISCES

SATURDAY, 19TH JUNE
Venus square Saturn

Though your personal inclinations point you in the direction of frivolity, there's far too much to do to give in to such time-wasting notions. There's a mountain of tasks to be tackled so it's a nose to the grindstone day. A woman may seem out of sorts and irritable… perhaps you aren't paying her enough attention?

SUNDAY, 20TH JUNE
Sun sextile Jupiter

If you've got any big ideas about bringing out the full potential of your home, but have been held back by a lack of cash, then help is at hand. The aspect between the Sun and Jupiter promises that money is on its way that will at least help you towards your goal. In all domestic affairs from redecoration to moving house, the influence of these two powerful bodies makes this a day when luck smiles on you and yours. A relative may be a benefactor to make your dream come true.

MONDAY, 21ST JUNE
Sun into Cancer

You are going to be in a slightly frivolous frame of mind over the next few weeks and you shouldn't punish yourself for this. Pay attention to a creative interest or a demanding hobby now or get involved in something creative on behalf of others. A couple of typical examples would be the production of a school play or making preparations for a flower and vegetable show.

TUESDAY, 22ND JUNE
Venus opposite Uranus

You're likely to be moody and unpredictable today. Not only will others find your constant changes of mind and feelings difficult to cope with, you too will irritate yourself. You could be overwrought and in need of some peace and quiet to calm down.

WEDNESDAY, 23RD JUNE
Mercury square Mars

Your lover may be putting too much pressure on you in some practical way and it is also possible that your other half is expecting far too great a financial contribution from you now. You simply cannot go on handing out money for extravagances or being expected to come up with lavish and luxurious holidays when you are struggling to make ends meet.

PISCES

THURSDAY, 24TH JUNE
Moon opposite Saturn

If you're off on your travels today then be prepared to put up with some delays and detours along the way. Nothing really can go exactly to plan at the moment since the stressful influence of Saturn is out to disrupt your well-ordered plans. Difficulties must be borne with patience now.

FRIDAY, 25TH JUNE
Mercury square Jupiter

As far as money is concerned, you are something of a wastrel today. A spendthrift impulse takes a hold and no amount of common sense will stop you from splashing out. Though theoretically you know that your reserves aren't limitless, you aren't inclined to rein in the spending. I should lock away your credit cards before it's too late.

SATURDAY, 26TH JUNE
Mercury into Leo

The movement of Mercury into your Solar sixth house of work, duties and health suggests that a slightly more serious phase is on the way. Over the next three weeks or so you will have to concentrate on what needs to be done rather than on having a good time. You may have a fair bit to do with neighbours, colleagues and relatives of around your own age group soon and you will have to spend a fair bit of time on the phone to them.

SUNDAY, 27TH JUNE
Moon trine Venus

Your eyes are set on the professional stars and you aren't the only one whose sure that they are attainable. Your partner, friends and colleagues have full confidence in you, and will be all too willing to assist in any small way to your eventual success.

MONDAY, 28TH JUNE
Jupiter into Taurus

Jupiter moves into its least happy position today, as it enters your Solar third house. Here the exuberance and optimism of the giant planet is somewhat muted by a tendency not to see other people's points of view. Your mind will be very active, but even though you'll easily accumulate facts you may not be able to put the lessons of life to their best use.

PISCES

TUESDAY, 29TH JUNE
Moon trine Saturn

It's good to have supportive friends. When you are anxious a few wise words from an experienced person can set your mind at rest. Be open about your aims, ambitions and fears today and you'll find that those around you will offer help and friendly advice.

WEDNESDAY, 30TH JUNE
Mercury opposite Neptune

Don't take on anything too demanding today. The planet of the mind is totally confused by an opposition to Neptune so you're likely to be very vague indeed. Leave anything important till tomorrow.

July at a Glance

LOVE	❤	❤	❤	❤	
WORK	★	★	★	★	★
MONEY	£				
HEALTH	✪	✪	✪	✪	✪
LUCK	♘	♘	♘	♘	♘

THURSDAY, 1ST JULY
Moon sextile Pluto

You are beginning to build up useful contacts which will help you to achieve your future aims and aspirations outside of the home. You may have some kind of secret goal in mind now, or it may be that you are just not ready to advertise this just yet. If so, you can move slowly and subtly towards this end while keeping your long-term intentions close to your chest.

FRIDAY, 2ND JULY
Moon opposite Venus

Emotional anxieties come to the fore today, but if you were honest you'd have to admit that you're being slightly neurotic over this. It's all the fault of the Lunar opposition to Venus which has managed to both heighten your emotional vulnerability and sap your energy levels at the same time. This problem of

PISCES

tiredness occurs again and again so perhaps a visit to your medical practitioner would be in order.

SATURDAY, 3RD JULY
Moon trine Mars

It's about time you showed that you are a formidable contender in the rat race, and today's Lunar aspect to Mars ensures that you'll do just that. No longer will you be content to play second fiddle or to put up with second best. You have a good idea of what you want and will be determined to get it. Speak up and make your presence felt.

SUNDAY, 4TH JULY
Mars opposite Jupiter

Take care while travelling today. If you can avoid taking any kind journey now you would be doing yourself a favour. However, if you must travel, then allow extra time for delays, breakdowns and other frustrations.

MONDAY, 5TH JULY
Mars into Scorpio

Today, Mars will move into the area of your chart which is devoted to expansion of horizons. This could herald a period of travel to new and interesting places or meeting and making friends with people who come from a different kind of background to yourself. This may be the start of one of those phases where you have to deal with legalities or with official matters of some kind.

TUESDAY, 6TH JULY
Moon square Sun

Go easy on your expenditure today. Avoid the shops, don't go looking for bargains and don't let anybody else talk you into buying anything either. Older relatives may be a bit irritating today, possibly because they need you to do something for them which eats into your spare time. It would be better to spend today attending to your duties rather than to seek out amusements.

WEDNESDAY, 7TH JULY
Moon trine Venus

An office romance or a chance meeting at work which turns into love is quite possible from today onwards! Even if this is not the case, you could enjoy a gentle flirtation with the delivery girl or the man who calls round to your workplace. There should be goodwill and kindness around you both at work and among any people whom you work with in a voluntary capacity.

PISCES

THURSDAY, 8TH JULY
Mercury trine Pluto

You can get your own way in work affairs as long as you are subtle about it. This is not a time to come straight out with a suggestion or a request. You have to work your way around it, dropping hints here and there. Bosses and colleagues will soon get the message because you are a consummate manipulator now.

FRIDAY, 9TH JULY
Moon square Venus

You may be feeling mentally or physically under the weather today. Your usual vigour seems to have deserted you and your zest for life has vanished off the face of the earth. Friends who should be repaying your past goodness by looking after you also seem to be doing a vanishing act. All in all, a rotten day.

SATURDAY, 10TH JULY
Moon sextile Mercury

Good news! If you are waiting for something to be fixed at home or at work, it will be. Frustrations will melt away as friends, neighbours and relatives rush round to help out with all those minor chores and problems that are plaguing you. A neighbourhood event may provide some unexpected amusement and pals who pop in may provide some more.

SUNDAY, 11TH JULY
Mars square Neptune

You aren't at your sharpest today being in a more dreamy and rather vague frame of mind. Unfortunately demands will be placed upon you. Be warned though, any decision made now will turn out to be mistaken in some way, especially if it's made under pressure. Try to isolate yourself from others as much as possible.

MONDAY, 12TH JULY
Mercury retrograde

Everything comes to a dead stop in your working environment as Mercury again pauses in his course. News of opportunities may now be delayed. Letters, phone calls and professional contacts are either mistimed or full of evasion. Don't worry, this period will pass.

TUESDAY, 13TH JULY
New Moon

There's a New Moon today casting a glow over your artistic potential. Your talents should shine now so have some belief in yourself and in what you can offer

PISCES

to the world at large. Of course if art and literature leave you cold, you may be more inclined to an amorous path. Conventional values are not for you now since you're determined to be yourself and to chart your own course. Make time to have fun, you deserve it.

WEDNESDAY, 14TH JULY
Moon conjunct Mercury

When the Moon makes contact with Mercury the mental powers are enhanced. You're very sharp now especially when you have to deal with any technicalities of life. If you're dealing with tradesmen, plumbers, domestic engineers and the like, you're very sharp. Unfortunately since the Solar house of health is also activated you may be prone to hypochondria today. More realistically, you may even suffer from some allergy or other. If in doubt consult your doctor.

THURSDAY, 15TH JULY
Venus trine Jupiter

The lines of communication will be very clear today, especially between you and your partner. It will be easy to get your point of view across and there will be no need to do this in an unpleasant or nagging manner. This is also a great day for financial dealings of all kinds, especially if you have something to sell.

FRIDAY, 16TH JULY
Mercury trine Pluto

Today's outlook is work-oriented. You will gain a vision of the possibilities that await you, as Pluto and Mercury open your eyes to your own potentials. You will be developing a strong ambition that you will be capable of achieving.

SATURDAY, 17TH JULY
Void Moon

The Moon is 'void of course' today, so don't bother with anything important and don't start anything new now. Stick to your usual routines and don't change your lifestyle in any way.

SUNDAY, 18TH JULY
Saturn square Uranus

You may be tricked or forced into an admission today. Confidences can and will slip out if you are not extremely careful. Choose your companions with great care and remember that if in doubt say nothing at all!

PISCES

MONDAY, 19TH JULY
Moon trine Uranus

A brainwave that could revolutionize a future project fills your mind and heart with glee. If you're wise you'll keep this information to yourself now, because there are folk around who wouldn't think twice about pinching your ideas and leaving you out in the cold. You are a trusting soul as a rule, but if someone starts asking too many questions about your projects now, it would be wise to keep some of the information back.

TUESDAY, 20TH JULY
Moon square Sun

Though you're still in the mood for fun and adventure, those close to home don't appreciate your apparently selfish actions. A money worry may emerge today, which will do nothing to encourage any harmony. Very little can be resolved today so wait until this stellar influence passes.

WEDNESDAY, 21ST JULY
Jupiter square Neptune

Though you have an uncanny knack of hitting the nail on the head today, you may be quite tactless when you try to communicate your insights. Be that as it may, it's sometimes more important to be truthful than diplomatic.

THURSDAY, 22ND JULY
Mercury square Mars

Once you see your situation clearly, it's too easy to irritate you with hidebound attitudes and narrow-minded views. You are in the fortunate position for seeing the way forward without confusion or being distracted by irrelevancies; unfortunately those around you don't have the benefit of your keen perception. It would be best to patiently explain your intentions… if, that is, you can be bothered to spend time with those who are out of tune with your thoughts.

FRIDAY, 23RD JULY
Sun into Leo

The Sun moves into your Solar sixth house of work and duty for the next month. This Solar movement will also encourage you to concentrate on your health and well-being and also that of your family. If you are off-colour, the Sun will help you to get back to full health once again. If you have jobs that need to be done, the next month or so will be a good time to get them done.

PISCES

SATURDAY, 24TH JULY
Moon sextile Uranus

There could be an unexpected break which helps you to achieve one particular ambition today. There are also some rather good long-term trends now which help you on the way to reaching your more distant objectives. You may have to do some lateral thinking in order to sort out a problem at work but your mind is working overtime now, and you will be able to come up with just the right amount of ingeniousness to solve this.

SUNDAY, 25TH JULY
Mercury square Jupiter

Your thinking may be muddled today and any decisions that you take could be quite wrong. Don't sign anything important and don't agree to anything where money or business is concerned. You are not in possession of the full facts and you will pay the price for any impetuosity that you display at this time. Take a cool, calm and long-term view of any business, financial or legal matters.

MONDAY, 26TH JULY
Sun opposite Neptune

There is likely to be a good deal of chaos around you today and this will be especially noticeable in your place of work. You could be anxious about real or imagined problems and the whole atmosphere seems to be one of jittery uncertainty. You may be tempted to strike out against others now but it would be best to wait for the situation (and also your own strange mood) to settle down again before saying or doing anything that you might regret.

TUESDAY, 27TH JULY
Sun square Jupiter

Money that is owning to you may be uncomfortably late in arriving, so don't bother looking for it in the post today! Obstacles may be placed in your way at work and it will be hard to get other people to see things with the same sense of urgency that you do. You may be frustrated by someone in a position of responsibility who seems to have a slow and philosophical attitude to what you see as urgent.

WEDNESDAY, 28TH JULY
Full Moon eclipse

Today's Eclipse concentrates on your working life and shows you that it may be time to call a halt to any activity that isn't giving you sufficient rewards or satisfaction. If your health's been troubling you then it's time to get the problem sorted out once and for all. Ignoring an ache won't make it go away. If you have

PISCES

any fears on this score then surely it's better to check everything out if only to set your mind at rest. Perhaps the only true cure to health worries and work concerns is a complete change of routine.

THURSDAY, 29TH JULY
Moon square Saturn

It pains you when you want to help out with advice and guidance but those who need it most won't listen to common sense. Some times it's better to let people just get on with it while you sit back. You can't impose solutions on others you know, they must be ready to accept offers of aid. I'm sure the subject of your concern will see sense eventually, until then be patient.

FRIDAY, 30TH JULY
Sun trine Pluto

If you are in a position of responsibility you will find that you have a difficult task to do today. However, it is a measure of the respect in which you are held by your colleagues that you have been given this job in the first place. You can do it!

SATURDAY, 31ST JULY
Mercury retrograde

You may have to go back over some job that you thought you had completed and finalize a few more details. This is particularly likely in the case of any kind of creative or artistic work.

August at a Glance

LOVE	♥	♥	♥	♥	
WORK	★				
MONEY	£				
HEALTH	✛	✛	✛	✛	✛
LUCK	♘	♘			

SUNDAY, 1ST AUGUST
Moon trine Mercury

If you need help with your children, friends, neighbours and even relatives of

PISCES

around your own age will turn to and give you a hand. They will see that you are struggling and they will reach out to help you. Children and young people will turn out to be a source of pleasure and of inspiration today and, all in all, you will feel uplifted rather than harassed by them now.

MONDAY, 2ND AUGUST
Moon trine Sun

It's a good day for dealing with documents, papers and official forms. Gather all information together so that you can work out the state of your finances now because it'll solve no end of hassles later. It doesn't matter if you're dealing in petty cash or millions the principle is the same and forethought now could save you a lot in the future.

TUESDAY, 3RD AUGUST
Venus trine Jupiter

Your spending may go through the roof as Venus and Jupiter take the brakes off your self-restraint today. Thrift may be forgotten but fun is at the top of your personal agenda, especially if you are in the company with the one you love!

WEDNESDAY, 4TH AUGUST
Moon trine Venus

Social opportunities are all around you now, so don't sit around on you own when there are people out there who'd welcome your company. Pop into a neglected friend's for a cup of tea and a chat, you'll be glad you made the effort as well as cheering up someone who needs it. Pick up the phone and ring a distant friend or one or two of your relatives for a good old gossip today.

THURSDAY, 5TH AUGUST
Moon conjunct Saturn

The Moon teams up with Saturn today endowing you with considerable self-discipline and a capacity for hard mental work. You have the ability to sit down and concentrate deeply now. No problem is beyond you. In social interactions, a more serious side to your character will emerge.

FRIDAY, 6TH AUGUST
Mercury direct

You should try to stretch your mind by pitting your wits against a problem or two now. There is no need for this to be a serious matter; it may simply be a case of doing a couple of crosswords, enjoying a game of chess or scrabble, or doing something more energetic, such as enjoying a game of snooker or badminton.

PISCES

SATURDAY, 7TH AUGUST
Sun square Mars

More haste, less speed! That's the astral message as Sol and Mars team up in a fiery combination. The workday can't end quickly enough. Boring duties weigh heavily and your restless yearning for excitement won't give you any peace. You need some extra-mental stimulation to get you through the day. Just remember that snapping irritably at colleagues won't fulfil your needs.

SUNDAY, 8TH AUGUST
Sun opposite Uranus

Take care of your health today and try to avoid having silly accidents now. Also try to project a public image that is completely cool and in control. Under the surface, you may be boiling with rage or twitching with anxiety, but it is best to avoid showing this on the surface. You will need to maintain sane and sensible methods of doing things at work and you will have to behave in a particularly calm and sensible manner.

MONDAY, 9TH AUGUST
Moon sextile Saturn

You are in a business like frame of mind today, and even though it may take time, you'll work your way through the most intractable problem. A serious time spent with a loved one will deepen your affection.

TUESDAY, 10TH AUGUST
Sun square Saturn

You can be prone to pessimism sometimes so today's harsh aspect between the Sun and Saturn is not good news for your state of mind. The smallest setback at work, or the most minor ache will be blown out of proportion and plunge you into the depth of despair. If you were more realistic you'd realize that nothing is as serious as it seems. Blame your negative mood and at least attempt to sweep away this aura of gloom.

WEDNESDAY, 11TH AUGUST
New Moon eclipse

Even though Nostradamus reckons that this is the day of doom, Sasha and Jonathan are slightly more optimistic even if there is a Solar eclipse. This means that you will have to face up to the fact that something in your life needs to be changed. The evidence is that you need a change of job but you will need to look at your own personal birthchart in some detail in order to work out whether this is the real reason for your currently unsettled state of mind.

PISCES

THURSDAY, 12TH AUGUST
Mercury into Leo

Some monetary worries should be alleviated by Mercury's change of sign today. Of course, this does not come without effort and you may find that you have to take on a part-time job in the short term to get the books to balance. More generally, improvements in the job stakes are now possible, but you'll have to be keenly aware of the possible competition and prepared to act instantly to get the employment you want.

FRIDAY, 13TH AUGUST
Mercury opposite Neptune

Anxieties may cause some sort of psychosomatic ailment today. The influences of Neptune and Mercury connect both inner and outer problems. Try to relieve stress in some way and you'll find your ailment will go as mysteriously as is came.

SATURDAY, 14TH AUGUST
Mars opposite Saturn

It's one of those 'One step forward, two steps back' sort of days! Mars and Saturn are at odds which makes progress very difficult and adds to your sense of frustration. Patience isn't easy now, but you'd better try to develop some, otherwise you'll be extremely irritable.

SUNDAY, 15TH AUGUST
Venus retrograde

If you are suffering from lower back pain or a sore throat we shouldn't be at all surprised. Venus has moved backwards into your health area bringing with it some niggling little ailments. Nothing serious though, but irritating all the same.

MONDAY, 16TH AUGUST
Moon sextile Sun

You are in tune with your innermost self today. Whether you are involved in your daily round of duties or involved with the most complicated forms and financial arrangements you are clear-sighted and totally capable. Even with the most intimate matters, your tact, diplomacy and sense of inner truth will untangle the most complex knot.

TUESDAY, 17TH AUGUST
Mercury square Jupiter

Rumours are abounding at work, at home and just about everywhere else. If you believe all of these rumours you will end up worrying yourself into a sleepless

PISCES

night. Try to remain calm and unmoved by gossip and work to create a sense of positive self-belief.

WEDNESDAY, 18TH AUGUST
Moon opposite Saturn

If you're off on your travels today then be prepared to put up with some delays and detours along the way. Nothing really can go exactly to plan at the moment since the stressful influence of Saturn is out to disrupt your well-ordered plans. Difficulties must be borne with patience now.

THURSDAY, 19TH AUGUST
Pluto direct

Pluto turns to direct motion today. The part of your chart that this affects is devoted to your long-term aims and ambitions. You may have felt over the past few months that you are getting nowhere fast or that your personal goals were becoming harder to achieve. From now on you will notice a slow but sure improvement which makes it far easier for you to focus on your ambitions and, ultimately, to achieve them.

FRIDAY, 20TH AUGUST
Sun conjunct Venus

The astral vibes are pretty good when the Sun gets together with Venus. You feel on top of the world and ready for anything. The only problem is that you have such an appetite for the good life that you could easily overdo it. Have fun by all means but don't indulge yourself so much that you'll regret it in the morning.

SATURDAY, 21ST AUGUST
Moon trine Venus

Things are at last falling into place both in the career sense and within a close relationship. The Lunar aspect to Venus ensures a deep and abiding harmony developing which makes you a far more effective force in the workplace. As your emotional life settles into a pattern of contentment, you'll find that your career path will follow suit.

SUNDAY, 22ND AUGUST
Moon trine Jupiter

Friends will want to talk over some of their problems today and you will be happy to lend a listening ear. You may feel like off-loading some of your worries on them too and the whole exercise will help you to put things into perspective again. This is also a rather lucky day for money and a gamble may pay off now too.

PISCES

MONDAY, 23RD AUGUST
Sun into Virgo

The Sun moves into the area of your chart devoted to relationships from today. If things have been difficult in a partnership, either personal or in business, then this is your chance to put everything back into its proper place. It's obvious that the significant other in your life deserves respect and affection and that's just what you're now prepared to give. Teamwork is the key to success over the next month.

TUESDAY, 24TH AUGUST
Venus square Mars

The daily habits of life seem all too restricting and limited at the moment and you'll be looking for something to alleviate your boredom. You know that there's more to life than the usual grind and will be anxious for new experience and stimulation. It's unfortunate that your self-expression suffers from this mood so try not to be too negative or sarcastic to those around you.

WEDNESDAY, 25TH AUGUST
Jupiter retrograde

You will notice a slowing down in many of your affairs now. Business matters will take their time and any negotiations that you are involved in could become complicated over the next few weeks.

THURSDAY, 26TH AUGUST
Full Moon

The Full Moon in your sign shows that you've come to the end of a personal phase and that it's time to tie up the loose ends and move on. This should be an opportunity to rid yourself of harmful little habits and create a whole new persona. This could be an image transformation. So, if you're at all dissatisfied by the way you present yourself to the world, then work out your own personal make-over. You'll be astounded by the reception the new you gets.

FRIDAY, 27TH AUGUST
Mercury conjunct Venus

You are beginning to realize that you must do something to polish up your image at work. Perhaps you need to improve your wardrobe and get your hair sorted out in order to look better. Maybe you need to make sure that your voice and your opinions are heard by those who matter.

PISCES

SATURDAY, 28TH AUGUST
Sun trine Jupiter

There will be good news for you and also for your lover today and this could bring extra money into the family coffers now. You may have a legal or an official matter to consider and this too will go rather well today. You should get on to people who have promised things and not got around to doing them yet because the chances are that you could get things moving along nicely now.

SUNDAY, 29TH AUGUST
Moon trine Pluto

You are being given a fantastic opportunity to set your feet on the stairway to supreme success in your aims and ambitions. Today's stars are edging you ever closer to your professional or social goals. Throw all your resources into an ambitious endeavour and watch your stars rise into the ascendant. You may be given a rise or an opportunity to earn more in the future.

MONDAY, 30TH AUGUST
Saturn retrograde

As Saturn goes retrograde from today, there's a need for some hard facts to be faced and some sober thinking to deal with them. You may feel that your education was insufficient for your present ambitions. If that's so, then look out for college courses to remedy your lack of knowledge or qualifications.

TUESDAY, 31ST AUGUST
Mercury into Virgo

The inquisitive Mercury moves into your Solar house of marriage and long-lasting relationships from today ushering in a period when a renewed understanding can be reached between yourself and your partner. New relationships can be formed under this influence too though these will tend to be on a light, fairly superficial level. Good humour and plenty of charm should be a feature for a few weeks, though you must try to curb a tendency to needlessly criticize another's foibles. Remember, not even you are perfect!

PISCES

September at a Glance

LOVE	❤				
WORK	★	★	★	★	★
MONEY	£	£	£	£	
HEALTH	✪	✪	✪	✪	
LUCK	♘	♘			

WEDNESDAY, 1ST SEPTEMBER
Moon square Venus

There seems to be quite a bit of pressure on you at work at the moment and the worst of the problem is that you don't know whom you can talk to and whom you should keep in the dark. A woman could cause you considerable problems today. Her motives may be quite pure but circumstances may make her act against your interests in some way.

THURSDAY, 2ND SEPTEMBER
Mars into Sagittarius

It's now time for drive, force and ambition as Mars enters the career area encouraging you to forge ahead with plans. You may feel you want to take a more independent course so this influence favours those who run their own businesses. You'll be very brash and forthright.

FRIDAY, 3RD SEPTEMBER
Mercury trine Jupiter

This is a good time to get down to a long talk with your partner about your future strategy. You may decide on a sensible budget now or you may decide that you can afford to spend a little more on luxuries such as travel or visiting friends. You and your loved ones may get involved in some kind of sporting activity soon and this would be successful for you on many different levels.

SATURDAY, 4TH SEPTEMBER
Mercury square Pluto

You will feel today that power is slipping from your grasp. If you are trying to deal with a tricky relationship situation or if you are trying to achieve something

PISCES

important in your working life, or both, you will feel that you just can't get things right. Whatever you say will 'come out wrong' and you will appear to be unsympathetic, manipulative or even power-grabbing even though none of these options is intended.

SUNDAY, 5TH SEPTEMBER
Moon sextile Saturn

Travelling for fun is the order of the day. Fun is not a concept usually associated with Saturn, but today you can use your time planning an excursion that you know you will enjoy. The company of an older brother or sister is possible too.

MONDAY, 6TH SEPTEMBER
Mars sextile Neptune

Follow your instincts now and you won't go far wrong! An inspiration should be acted upon immediately, even if others think that you are totally wrong. Your gut feelings are a better judge of reality at the moment!

TUESDAY, 7TH SEPTEMBER
Moon opposite Uranus

Your unconscious mind has a number of tricks up its sleeve at the moment and you should try not to ignore suppressed emotions because the stress from these could make you ill. You need to work out what is at the root of your uneasiness and, if at all possible, do something about it. It may be worth looking back over your life and analysing the past in order to find the key to your future happiness.

WEDNESDAY, 8TH SEPTEMBER
Sun conjunct Mercury

You and your lover have a great deal to talk over and today is the day to do it. If you are in the early stages of a relationship, you will find that you have a great deal in common and you will be able to while away many happy hours together discussing your childhoods and backgrounds. If you have something that is niggling you, you should not keep this to yourself because it will linger there, possibly causing long-term resentment.

THURSDAY, 9TH SEPTEMBER
New Moon

The only planetary activity today is a new Moon in your opposite sign. It is possible that this could bring the start of a new relationship for the lonely but, to be honest, this planetary aspect is a bit too weak for such a big event. Better to improve on a current relationship rather than to start a new one at this time.

PISCES

FRIDAY, 10TH SEPTEMBER
Sun trine Saturn

No matter in what rosy light you like to view your love life, the Sun's aspect to Saturn shows that there is some work to be done in a close relationship. At least this aspect is a good one so some constructive communication can go a long way to resolving points of difficulty. A serious talk about your ambitions and ideas will open a whole new understanding of what you're about in your partner's eyes.

SATURDAY, 11TH SEPTEMBER
Venus direct

You should find the atmosphere at work much more pleasant now that Venus has moved into that area of your chart. You may be moved to another working area that is much nicer. If you are housebound, then you can treat yourself to some kind of useful gadget for the home.

SUNDAY, 12TH SEPTEMBER
Moon sextile Venus

What a romantic and loving day this is! However, you are in such a soppy mood that you may find yourself agreeing to do something for your lover that, under other, more sober circumstances, you would never have agreed to at all.

MONDAY, 13TH SEPTEMBER
Moon square Neptune

A vague, dreamy sort of day in which very little will be accomplished simply because you won't be in the mood. You'd be happiest in solitude thinking beautiful thoughts without any intrusions of the harsh world.

TUESDAY, 14TH SEPTEMBER
Moon opposite Saturn

You could be irritated by the entrenched prejudices of a relative or neighbour today! Calm, reasoned argument will do nothing to dent the rock-hard opinions you encounter! The worst thing is that, though you'll be in the right, there is nothing you can do to change anyone else's mind! Try to take it philosophically!

WEDNESDAY, 15TH SEPTEMBER
Mars conjunct Pluto

If you have been in a kind of backwater or if your life has been drifting along over the last few weeks, today's events will help to put it back onto the right track. You may have to fight with someone over who wields the power either at work or at home because others may have been trying to undermine your position.

PISCES

THURSDAY, 16TH SEPTEMBER
Mercury into Libra

Mercury moves into one of the most sensitive areas of your chart from today. Anything of an intimate nature from your physical relationships to the state of your bank balance comes under scrutiny now. Turn your heightened perceptions to your love life, important partnerships, and any affair that deals with investment, insurance, tax or shared resources. An intelligent approach now will save you a lot of problems later.

FRIDAY, 17TH SEPTEMBER
Mercury trine Neptune

Psychic, supernatural and occult interests dominate your mind today and you seem to be entranced by any subject which is out of the ordinary and you are particularly drawn to anything that exudes an aura of magic and mystery. You may be keen to find out how unusual people's minds work and this may lead you to read books or watch videos on strange, spooky or even violent subjects.

SATURDAY, 18TH SEPTEMBER
Moon square Mercury

You may have to cancel an arrangement with a friend today, possibly due to having to run a few important errands for your partner or for your working colleagues. If you need to go to the bank or the post office, allow plenty of time to get there or for waiting in the queue when you arrive. This is especially important if you have something more than the usual simple transaction to deal with.

SUNDAY, 19TH SEPTEMBER
Moon trine Saturn

You'll be in a very serious frame of mind today, with no time for frivolous gossip or idle people. You'll be busy thinking of intellectual matters, and many will be planning a celebration that will take a lot of organizing.

MONDAY, 20TH SEPTEMBER
Moon trine Sun

There is great news today in connection with a partnership or a relationship. If money has been an obstacle to your love, then this problem could soon be solved. A friend may act as a go-between in order to keep you in contact with those who matter to you.

PISCES

TUESDAY, 21ST SEPTEMBER
Mercury sextile Pluto

You are at your most subtle today. You know that the direct approach is not going to work with anything that smacks of officialdom. Fortunately you are cunning enough to use the roundabout route in getting what you want.

WEDNESDAY, 22ND SEPTEMBER
Moon opposite Venus

You must take care of your nerves and of your health today. There is no danger of accidents but you could be feeling a bit low and you might be vulnerable to infection. Stay away from cold wet places and try to rest as much as you can. You may have some difficulty with a female colleague at work, possibly because she is under the weather. If so, don't try to do all her work as well as your own.

THURSDAY, 23RD SEPTEMBER
Sun into Libra

Today, the Sun enters your Solar eighth house of beginnings and endings. Thus, over the next month, you can expect something to wind its way to a conclusion, while something else starts to take its place. This doesn't seem to signify a major turning point or any really big event in your life but it does mark one of those small turning points that we all go through from time to time.

FRIDAY, 24TH SEPTEMBER
Mars sextile Uranus

Career affairs may be moving too slowly for your comfort today so you'll be quite prepared to put a rocket under people who are more sedate than you. If you can't get the results you want under the influences of Mars and Uranus, then you aren't trying!

SATURDAY, 25TH SEPTEMBER
Full Moon

Today's full Moon seems to be highlighting a minor problem in connection with financial matters. You may have been overspending recently and this could be the cause of your current financial embarrassment but there does seem to be something deeper to be considered here. Perhaps the firm you work for has a temporary problem or maybe your partner is a bit short of cash just now.

SUNDAY, 26TH SEPTEMBER
Moon opposite Mercury

You are far too emotional to make any sort of truly sensible decision today.

PISCES

You've got some intimate affair constantly at the back of your mind so when it comes to finances and the best use of cash leave it to another day when you can weigh up the pros and cons more effectively.

MONDAY, 27TH SEPTEMBER
Moon square Neptune

This is not a day for solitude. Too much time on your own will give you a grim outlook and make you prone to morbid fancies. Talk your worries over with a good friend. A problem shared is a problem halved.

TUESDAY, 28TH SEPTEMBER
Moon conjunct Saturn

Frivolous people and time wasters will get short shrift from you today because you've got far more weighty matters on your mind. You simply can't be bothered with trivialities when the world seems such a demanding place and time is at such a premium. Your instincts are on course and you know that it's best to get your head down and carry your tasks through to the end. This is especially true if you're planning journeys or involved in educational affairs.

WEDNESDAY, 29TH SEPTEMBER
Moon trine Neptune

A misty look is apparent in your eye as a dreamy frame of mind overtakes the more common-sense aspects of your personality. You'll be extremely nostalgic, with more than a touch of rose-tinted spectacles about your happy memories.

THURSDAY, 30TH SEPTEMBER
Moon trine Uranus

There seems to be a number of unexpected events going on in and around your home and family now. There could be news of a family celebration or two and even an unusual reconciliation of some kind. If you have done good turns to family members in the past, these obligations could now be paid back to you. You may find some kind of interesting item for your home now.

PISCES

October at a Glance

LOVE	♥	♥	♥	♥
WORK	★	★		
MONEY	£			
HEALTH	✪	✪	✪	
LUCK	U	U		

FRIDAY, 1ST OCTOBER
Sun sextile Pluto

This is a chance to show off your leadership qualities. People at work will look to you for guidance, but it may not be wise to reveal all that you know! Financially, things are looking better with the chance of profit in the offing; however, here too discretion is important.

SATURDAY, 2ND OCTOBER
Mercury sextile Venus

Your mind and your heart seem to be working in harmony today. You seem to be blessed with a silver tongue and the art of diplomacy now, so use this talent to sort out any difficulties between others today.

SUNDAY, 3RD OCTOBER
Moon square Mercury

Any agreements concerning such sensitive issues as inheritance, investments or even alimony will go nowhere if you give in to an emotional outburst today. Feelings are running high, so it's more important than ever than you keep a cool head. Don't let your heart intrude into matters of finance.

MONDAY, 4TH OCTOBER
Moon sextile Sun

If you need to find the right person to do a particular job for you, you should be able to do this with ease today. Your mood is good now and you have the happy inner feeling that you are on the right track in many areas of your life.

PISCES

TUESDAY, 5TH OCTOBER
Mercury into Scorpio

Mercury enters your Solar house of adventure and philosophy from today and stimulates your curiosity. Everything from international affairs to religious questions will tax your mind. Your desire to travel will be boosted for a few weeks, as indeed will a need to expand your knowledge, perhaps by taking up a course at a local college. Keep an open mind. Allow yourself encounters with new ideas.

WEDNESDAY, 6TH OCTOBER
Sun trine Uranus

You could be for a spot of luck in one or two of the more important areas of your life. Business matters could suddenly bring the kind of financial results that you need, while loving relationships will begin to work the way you want. Business or personal partnerships will be aided by a change in circumstances which seem to help your partner more than yourself, but this will turn out to have a beneficial knock-on effect on your own life.

THURSDAY, 7TH OCTOBER
Venus into Virgo

Venus, the planet of romance moves into your horoscope area of close relationships from today increasing your physical desires and bringing the light of love into your heart. If you're involved in a long-term partnership it's a chance to renew the magic of the early days of your union. If single, then the next few weeks should bring a stunning new attraction into your life.

FRIDAY, 8TH OCTOBER
Moon trine Neptune

You may want to help out a friend whose emotional state is making him or her vulnerable and unhappy. Your own feelings could be rather confused too but you are more likely to be inexplicably happy rather than downhearted. You may have a sudden flash of insight which helps you to solve some kind of outstanding problem either on your own behalf or on behalf of someone else.

SATURDAY, 9TH OCTOBER
New Moon

Apart from a new Moon today, there are no major planetary happenings. This suggests that you avoid making major changes in your life just now but make a couple of fresh starts in very minor matters. You may feel like taking your partner to task over his or her irritating ways, but perhaps today is not the best day for doing this.

PISCES

SUNDAY, 10TH OCTOBER
Venus trine Jupiter

All you'll have on your mind is fun with a capital F today! Thoughts of expense and duty are put aside as you decide to treat yourself and a loved one to a treat… And the way you feel, the more expensive the treat the better! Oh well, it doesn't happen that often, does it?

MONDAY, 11TH OCTOBER
Jupiter square Neptune

You may have something of vital importance to say yet you won't have much of an opportunity to say it today! The square aspect between Jupiter and Neptune will tend to frustrate your efforts at communication.

TUESDAY, 12TH OCTOBER
Void Moon

This is not a great day in which to decide anything or to start anything new. A void Moon suggests that there are no major planetary aspects being made, either between planets or involving the Sun or the Moon. This is a fairly unusual situation but it does happen from time to time and the only way to deal with it is to stick to your usual routines and do nothing special for a while.

WEDNESDAY, 13TH OCTOBER
Mercury square Uranus

It's very likely that you'll take on too much today. You may feel your conscience pricking you and this will spur you on to overload your schedule. Nervous tension too is likely, so try to take things easy or at least one at a time.

THURSDAY, 14TH OCTOBER
Neptune direct

Neptune returns to a more direct course from today bringing an almost psychic awareness into your life. From now on, spare some time to listen to the inner voice of intuition. It won't let you down.

FRIDAY, 15TH OCTOBER
Moon conjunct Mars

You may find yourself fighting with bureaucrats, officious officials, paranoid plutocrats or a parking meter attendant. There is only so far you can get with this but there is no need for you to be pushed around. Perhaps a strongly worded letter to the right place will do the trick in straightening things out for you now.

PISCES

SATURDAY, 16TH OCTOBER
Mercury opposite Saturn

Though your mind is full of bright ideas and new inspirations, when you come to explain them, you'll find that it all comes out wrongly. The mind is like a grasshopper leaping from leaf to leaf, you're rushing ahead of yourself so fast that there's the danger of seeming like a complete scatterbrain. Try to slow down and set out your arguments in a logical form. Failing that, keep a notebook handy so you don't forget any of your stunning ideas.

SUNDAY, 17TH OCTOBER
Mars into Capricorn

Friends are likely to be a strong influence on you at this time. Old friends may have interesting ideas to put your way, while new ones could come crowding into your life quite quickly now. You may join some kind of very active group who share your interests and are keen to have you as part of their organization. This may have something to do with sports or some other kind of energetic or outdoor activity.

MONDAY, 18TH OCTOBER
Venus square Pluto

All relationships need a little space in them if they are to flourish; however you could be feeling rather insecure at the moment and will want to cling to your other half like a limpet. Try to back off a little and trust to the strength and stability of your partnership!

TUESDAY, 19TH OCTOBER
Moon square Saturn

We're afraid that there's a fairly depressing influence about the Lunar aspect to Saturn today. It won't take much effort to think about all the things that possibly could go wrong in your life. The old enemy pessimism is back with a vengeance. Perhaps the cause of your worry is an elderly neighbour, or even closer, a brother or sister who is having considerable problems. Try to be calm and look on the bright side.

WEDNESDAY, 20TH OCTOBER
Moon sextile Jupiter

Today should be quite pleasant and there may even be a bit of extra money in the offing for you. You may hear from a friend or a relative who is at a distance from you or you may find yourself on a pleasant journey now.

PISCES

THURSDAY, 21ST OCTOBER
Moon opposite Venus

Someone very close to you is feeling a terrible burden of insecurity now. It may be that some harsh facts recently faced have shaken confidence. Some reassurance from you is now vital. Remember that you too can be prone to over-sensitivity so have some sympathy with one who needs your presence now.

FRIDAY, 22ND OCTOBER
Sun square Neptune

You are buzzing with bright ideas and promising schemes but it may be hard to bring them into manifestation. You may feel that others have it in for you or that nobody wants to see anything from your point of view. This is probably a touch of galloping paranoia, but there may be more than a little truth in your fears, because someone may indeed be saying or doing nasty things behind your back.

SATURDAY, 23RD OCTOBER
Sun into Scorpio

The Sun moves into your Solar ninth house today and it will stay there for a month. This would be a good time to travel overseas or to explore new neighbourhoods. It is also a good time to take up an interest in spiritual matters. You may find yourself keen to read about religious or philosophical subjects or even to explore the world of psychic healing over the next month or so.

SUNDAY, 24TH OCTOBER
Full Moon

This is likely to be a really awkward day for the kind of travelling that you have to do. A vehicle could let you down just when you most need it or the public transport that you usually rely on could suddenly disappear from the face of the earth.

MONDAY, 25TH OCTOBER
Venus trine Saturn

It's obvious that the aspect between Venus and Saturn denotes a make-or-break time in a relationship. It may be that you've passed the stage of airy romanticism and will now be considering the pros and cons of continuing a relationship. Whatever your decision, this will change your life.

TUESDAY, 26TH OCTOBER
Moon opposite Mercury

Your wonderfully logical, practical and sensible brain is on strike today. You will just not be able to think straight or to come up with a sensible answer to anything

PISCES

today, so don't try for the time being. Leave any important decisions until the stars have moved into a better position. It is not a good day to sign anything important either.

WEDNESDAY, 27TH OCTOBER
Moon opposite Pluto

You may be setting off hot-foot in pursuit of a terrific professional prize just now, but first you must concentrate on sorting out a domestic squabble or something that isn't working for you in the home area of your life. Your feelings are running very deeply now and you may be walking around with a great deal of unresolved anger or some other kind of unexpressed feelings.

THURSDAY, 28TH OCTOBER
Mercury sextile Neptune

Although your mood is dreamy and rather impractical, there is nothing wrong with your intuition. You will be able to get on well at work, mainly through feeling the atmosphere and making all your moves in an intuitive manner. Some of you will concentrate on spiritual or intuitive subjects today and, indeed, this would be an excellent day in which to start studying astrology.

FRIDAY, 29TH OCTOBER
Moon opposite Mars

Boredom is the enemy today because you're likely to react in an impulsive and even destructive way to anything that holds you down. The fault lies with the Lunar opposition to Mars which gives you irrepressible energy but limits your outlets. If your hobbies or leisure activities aren't giving you the satisfaction you crave, you should consider a new way to express yourself and regain some enthusiasm for life.

SATURDAY, 30TH OCTOBER
Mercury into Sagittarius

There's a certain flexibility entering your career structure as indicated by the presence of Mercury in your Solar area of ambition from today. You can now turn your acute mind to all sorts of career problems and solve them to everyone's satisfaction, and your own personal advantage. Your powers of persuasion will be heightened from now on, ensuring that you charm bosses and employers to get your own way. Those seeking work should attend interviews because your personality will shine.

PISCES

SUNDAY, 31ST OCTOBER
Moon square Sun

You may find it hard to concentrate on your usual chores today because other things seem to be intruding on your mind. It would be nice just to sit and dream or to stand gazing out of the window for an hour or so, but the chances are that you won't be able to do any of this. Your mind is full of interesting philosophical thoughts and ideas but the work also needs to be done.

November at a Glance

LOVE	♥	♥	♥	♥	♥
WORK	★	★	★	★	★
MONEY	£	£	£	£	
HEALTH	✪	✪	✪	✪	
LUCK	U	U	U	U	

MONDAY, 1ST NOVEMBER
Void Moon

Today is one of those odd days when there are no important planetary aspects being made, not even to the Moon. The best way to tackle these kinds of days is to stick to your usual routine and to avoid starting anything new or tackling anything of major importance. If you do decide to do something large today, it will take longer and be harder to cope with than it would normally.

TUESDAY, 2ND NOVEMBER
Moon square Mercury

If you want any peace now, you'd better keep your mouth firmly shut because you'll get very little sympathy or understanding now. The trouble is that you are pretty logical while those around you are too emotional to see anything rationally at all!

WEDNESDAY, 3RD NOVEMBER
Moon trine Saturn

A serious chat with your nearest and dearest will get your relationship back on an even keel once more. Talk over your worries, and remember to listen when your other half discusses his or her anxieties as well as your own.

PISCES

THURSDAY, 4TH NOVEMBER
Moon sextile Mercury

Check out the rumours that are travelling around your workplace. There may be talk of mergers and takeovers and of hiring and firings. Some of these may only be rumours but other bits of information may have some truth in them. On a more personal level, this is a good time to get passionate with your partner and to enjoy your favourite and sexiest amusements.

FRIDAY, 5TH NOVEMBER
Moon trine Uranus

You may receive a totally unexpected windfall today, possibly in the form of a tax rebate or from some other kind of governmental or official source. Your partner may have a bit of good luck which he or she shares with you. There could be an unexpected business break, a legal matter which suddenly goes your way or some other kind of unforeseen financial benefit.

SATURDAY, 6TH NOVEMBER
Sun opposite Saturn

A rather depressing day we're afraid when all the weight of the world seems to rest on your shoulders. Don't pressure yourself because there's enough pressure on you at the moment anyway. If thinking of travelling, save yourself a lot of hassle and stay at home!

SUNDAY, 7TH NOVEMBER
Sun sextile Mars

You'll find some friends are totally confused and in an emotional knot at the moment. Some straight talking from you can clear the air and throw new light on the worry that's perplexing them. You may be considered tactless but getting right to the point is far more useful than politeness now. If there's something to say you're the one to say it. They'll thank you eventually.

MONDAY, 8TH NOVEMBER
New Moon

The New Moon in your house of adventure urges you to push ahead with new projects. You're in a confident mood, and feel able to tackle anything the world throws at you. There's a lure of the exotic today as well, as far-off places exert a powerful attraction. Think again about widening your personal horizons, by travel or, indeed, by taking up an educational course. Intellectually you're on top form and your curiosity is boundless.

PISCES

TUESDAY, 9TH NOVEMBER
Mercury into Scorpio

You should take every opportunity that you can to gather facts, information, impressions and evidence today before going ahead with anything. You may have to deal with legal or official matters now and, if so, having all the right information to hand can only help. If there is nothing specific that you have to deal with, then just keep yourself informed of what is going on in your neighbourhood.

WEDNESDAY, 10TH NOVEMBER
Moon sextile Uranus

A disappointment may well turn out to be a blessing in disguise today. You may find yourself on a path that you had not previously considered, but one which will lead you to greater success than you imagined.

THURSDAY, 11TH NOVEMBER
Moon trine Jupiter

You can make real progress in all work-related affairs and in your ambitions today. The Moon is in splendid aspect to Jupiter showing that you are a talented and capable person. Luck is on your side so you'll find that people in authority will do their utmost to help you along your way. Be adaptable now, because fortune may not come in the way you expect.

FRIDAY, 12TH NOVEMBER
Moon square Venus

If you fancy an undemanding day with plenty of peace and harmony, we're afraid you're due for a rude awakening. No one has the slightest intention of leaving you to your own devices now. Well-meaning friends will urge you to be social, to get out and enjoy yourself but all they manage to do is make you irritable. If you really do crave solitude, you'll have to unplug the phone, not answer the door and pretend to be out.

SATURDAY, 13TH NOVEMBER
Moon conjunct Mars

Lonely ladies who are reading this have a terrific opportunity of meeting someone new today and it would happen in the most unexpected way. The rest of you can enjoy sporting activities or anything that you do with friends in a group or a social setting. Therefore, phone your friends and suggest a game of golf or something similar.

PISCES

SUNDAY, 14TH NOVEMBER
Saturn square Uranus

There are certain difficult issues to be faced up to today; unfortunately you won't be able to find the right words to do this. You'd better wait until a more favourable time before tackling anything too delicate!

MONDAY, 15TH NOVEMBER
Moon square Saturn

A fairly grim outlook for today as the Moon makes a bad aspect to Saturn. You'll be too inclined to look on the black side at the moment and need a change of scene to take your mind off your problems.

TUESDAY, 16TH NOVEMBER
Mercury sextile Mars

Sometimes the test of true friendship is the ability to tell the truth without worrying too much about the effect it has on a friend's feelings. This is one of those days when what you say will strike home and needs to be said. Of course it can be put nicely: there is no need for a confrontation over this.

WEDNESDAY, 17TH NOVEMBER
Venus sextile Pluto

Your love life should be taking off like a rocket today and you will have just what it takes to attract the attention of a fascinating new partner. If you already have a fascinating partner, you will know just how to keep his or her interest from flagging. If you want to get on at work now, put your heart into what you are doing, because there is no stopping your progress today.

THURSDAY, 18TH NOVEMBER
Moon trine Mercury

Things will move quickly today and anything that has been hanging in the air will now come down to earth and get itself sorted out very quickly. If you need to take advice on anything, whether this be an official matter, a visit to an astrologer or simply a chat to a friend, you will be able to find just the right person to help you today. You may take steps to learn something new or to gain some kind of useful skills today.

FRIDAY, 19TH NOVEMBER
Moon sextile Neptune

Follow your nose to a bargain today. If you are determined on a shopping trip, you'll find that you can sniff out the cheapest and best like a bloodhound. Don't

PISCES

worry too much about expense because anything you purchase will be well worth the cost.

SATURDAY, 20TH NOVEMBER
Venus trine Uranus

If you are in a settled relationship, surprise your partner by taking him or her out on a surprise outing, and the more imaginative and inventive this is, the better. Keep the spirit of love alive in your relationship by treating your lover to an unexpected gift or a little luxury now. If you are unattached, then put on your dancing shoes and try your luck at the local disco.

SUNDAY, 21ST NOVEMBER
Mars square Jupiter

With all the demands you've been putting on your system recently, we're not surprised that you're worn out. However, you may not actually feel too tired, but take it from me, your stress levels are too high for comfort so you'd be a fool to take on any more burdens. Well-meaning friends may invite you out, but really you don't need to socialize out of duty for that would only be a strain on your energy and your cash flow.

MONDAY, 22ND NOVEMBER
Sun into Sagittarius

The Sun moves decisively into your horoscope area of ambition from today bringing in a month when your worldly progress will achieve absolute priority. You need to feel that what you are doing is worthwhile and has more meaning than simply paying the bills. You may feel the urge to change you career, to make a long-term commitment to a worthwhile cause, or simply to demand recognition for past efforts. However this ambitious phase manifests you can be sure that your prospects are considerably boosted from now on.

TUESDAY, 23RD NOVEMBER
Full Moon

The Full Moon today focuses firmly on family and domestic issues. Perhaps it's time for some straight talking because this is the best opportunity you'll get to put an end to home-based or emotional problems. In some ways it's time to put your cards on the table, yet equally to give credit and take some share of blame in family affairs. Apart from such personal concerns it's time to speak to someone in authority about your ambitions.

PISCES

WEDNESDAY, 24TH NOVEMBER
Moon trine Venus

A truly romantic interlude could turn into real passion today. You seem to have the kind of magnetic charisma that's guaranteed to make you irresistible to the opposite sex. Even if all you end up doing is sitting about at home with your loved one, make this as sexy and loving an occasion as you can. Set the scene with perfume, dim lights and sexy music on the magic music machine tonight!

THURSDAY, 25TH NOVEMBER
Sun sextile Neptune

There may be a mix up in connection with your job, but this will come out in the wash soon enough. If you have a problem, someone will come to your aid, and it looks as if the person who gives you the most help operates at a surprisingly high level of authority. Other people will be happy to put your needs before their own for a change today.

FRIDAY, 26TH NOVEMBER
Mars into Aquarius

You seem to be entering a placid and peaceful backwater just now because Mars is disappearing into the quietest area of your chart. However, this is not quite true because you will spend this reflective time working out what you want from life and also making preparations for your future. This is a good time repay any loans or to fulfil any outstanding obligations towards others.

SATURDAY, 27TH NOVEMBER
Moon opposite Neptune

There's a very deceptive influence around you at the moment so it's important not to take anything at face value. Promises made now will not be kept so keep your tongue in your cheek.

SUNDAY, 28TH NOVEMBER
Moon square Mercury

Don't be too hard on yourself today. Accept that you have probably been working hard or that you have been under too much stress for your own good. Nobody can do everything and you are not superman (or superwoman, for that matter), so you shouldn't expect so much of yourself. You may have to spend some time with a colleague who is going through a crisis today.

PISCES

MONDAY, 29TH NOVEMBER
Mars conjunct Neptune

This is one of those days when your get up and go has got up and gone and although you are feeling rather restless and irritable, you can't really make anything gel yet. The fact is that your inner world of dreams and imagination is far more to your liking at the moment that the all-too-real world out there.

TUESDAY, 30TH NOVEMBER
Moon trine Saturn

It's time to talk things over with your partner. Problems have recently arisen and it's now the perfect opportunity to lay your cards on the table. This is not as drastic as it seems, because there will be a readiness to discuss issues sensibly on both sides.

December at a Glance

LOVE	♥	♥	♥	♥
WORK	★	★	★	★
MONEY	£	£	£	£
HEALTH	☉			
LUCK	♘			

WEDNESDAY, 1ST DECEMBER
Venus opposite Jupiter

You're in an extremely sensual frame of mind today with a taste for luxury. The opposition of Venus and Jupiter, while ensuring that nothing practical gets done, also makes you into a seductive and amorous creature. You've obviously got strong desires, but if sexual frolics aren't on offer, you could always indulge yourself with less intense temptations.

THURSDAY, 2ND DECEMBER
Moon sextile Sun

You may be faced with a bit of a battle today but your confidence is high and you seem to have an inner conviction that you can win. To be honest, we think that you are quite right!

PISCES

FRIDAY, 3RD DECEMBER
Moon opposite Jupiter

There's no point in making any far-reaching decisions in partnership or financial affairs today. You're too scatterbrained to make any sensible choices so just go with the flow. Don't allow blind optimism to get in the way of reason now.

SATURDAY, 4TH DECEMBER
Moon square Neptune

A dreamy and rather impractical mood prevails today. You won't be able to get much done simply because your heart won't be in it. We hope others aren't too demanding of you, because they'll be disappointed.

SUNDAY, 5TH DECEMBER
Venus into Scorpio

Venus enters your Solar ninth house of exploration this month and this may make you slightly restless. Venus is concerned with the pleasures of life and also with leisure activities of all kinds, so explore such ideas as your sporting interests, or perhaps of listening to interesting music or going to art galleries and the like. You may want to travel somewhere new and interesting soon.

MONDAY, 6TH DECEMBER
Sun sextile Uranus

A crusading zeal gets a grip of you today and you'll be full of fervour to change everything from your working practices to the world at large. You won't tolerate injustice or tyrannical attitudes from anyone and will be prepared to stand up for your rights!

TUESDAY, 7TH DECEMBER
New Moon

The new Moon today shows the great heights that you could possibly attain. The message is that there's nothing to fear except fear itself. Reach for the stars and you've got it made. Your career should begin to blossom now and you can achieve the kind of respect and status that you are looking for over the next month or so.

WEDNESDAY, 8TH DECEMBER
Venus square Neptune

It would be a good idea to take a break but don't try to do anything too energetic. Avoid making complicated travel plans today, because these would probably get fouled up, leaving you stranded in the middle of nowhere. Be careful whom you

PISCES

trust and be specifically wary of a woman who appears friendly but whom your instincts warn you about because your intuition will be right.

THURSDAY, 9TH DECEMBER
Moon sextile Venus

You're in a marvellously exuberant mood today. You need lots of stimulating company to keep you from the dreaded boredom so it's the more the merrier as far as you're concerned. The best bet is to arrange an informal gathering with your favourite people and take it from there.

FRIDAY, 10TH DECEMBER
Mars square Saturn

This is not going to be an easy day. The harsh aspect between Mars and Saturn shows that you are prone to self-doubt at the moment and your esteem is falling. You need something to distract you from this sombre frame of mind, so go out for a while because change of scene will do you good.

SATURDAY, 11TH DECEMBER
Mercury into Sagittarius

Your job will take precedence today and you must make an effort to get your voice heard. Fortunately, this will not be too difficult because your superiors and your colleagues will be reasonably ready to hear what you have to say. You may have some bright ideas in other areas of life today as well, and you shouldn't hesitate to put these into practice.

SUNDAY, 12TH DECEMBER
Mercury sextile Neptune

There is no keeping a good man (or woman) down today. You are determined to reach the top and you may find some pretty unconventional ways of doing so. Your level of intuition is amazingly high and you are almost bound to be receiving psychic messages from the world beyond at the moment. Take up something new and more technically advanced now because it could lead to a new and very productive career for you.

MONDAY, 13TH DECEMBER
Moon sextile Sun

Your mood is calm and you seem content to go along with what others want today. Fortunately, others seem to want much the same as you do, so there shouldn't be any conflicts of interests now.

PISCES

TUESDAY, 14TH DECEMBER
Mars conjunct Uranus

It looks as though this is likely to be a most unusual day, because old and loved friends could come sweeping unexpectedly back into your life now. You may suddenly decide to change your plans for the holidays, and take off with a friend for strange and distant shores. Even if you cannot actually do this, you can dream, can't you?

WEDNESDAY, 15TH DECEMBER
Venus opposite Saturn

Your brains will turn to jelly today! You will not be able to think straight or to make any kind of sensible decision. If you gamble, you will become the biggest loser going. If you play cards, you will be handed a deck that has no aces! The reason for this daftness could be due to a love affair that is taking up all your energy but it could just as easily have no real cause at all.

THURSDAY, 16TH DECEMBER
Moon sextile Neptune

Trust your instincts today because a hunch could lead you to profit. Money-making is the name of the game and your uncanny knack will help you considerably.

FRIDAY, 17TH DECEMBER
Sun trine Jupiter

There are a number of opportunities around you at the moment and you should take full advantage of this favourable trend. You may have to make some kind of adjustment to your aims and ambitions soon.

SATURDAY, 18TH DECEMBER
Mercury conjunct Pluto

You are the most persuasive person around today. The clarity and power of your arguments would sway the most stubborn person around to your way of thinking. In all career affairs, the ladder of success leads you onward and upward.

SUNDAY, 19TH DECEMBER
Moon conjunct Saturn

The Moon teams up with Saturn today endowing you with considerable self-discipline and a capacity for hard mental work. You have the ability to sit down and concentrate deeply now. No problem is beyond you. In social interactions, a more serious side to your character will emerge.

PISCES

MONDAY, 20TH DECEMBER
Jupiter into Aries

As Jupiter moves into your area of monetary good fortune, the planet of luck indicates that a period of material well-being is in the offing. The planet's happy-go-lucky influence will bring funds to you with an ease that you hadn't expected. However, throughout this period, you are unlikely to be much of a saver.

TUESDAY, 21ST DECEMBER
Moon opposite Pluto

The chores are chasing you from pillar to post and you may begin to feel that you have taken on the twelve labours of Hercules! If there is any way that you can speed this process up then do so. If you really do find a clever way of coping, send the answer to Sasha and Jonathan in an essay of no more than 500 words, because we would love to know how to do this for ourselves!

WEDNESDAY, 22ND DECEMBER
Sun into Capricorn

As the Sun makes its yearly entrance into your eleventh Solar house, you can be sure that friends and acquaintances are going to have a powerful influence on your prospects. The Sun's harmonious angle to your own sign gives an optimism and vitality to your outgoing nature. Social life will increase in importance over the next month. You'll be a popular and much sought-after person. Obstacles that have irritated you will now be swept away.

THURSDAY, 23RD DECEMBER
Full Moon

Today's Full Moon occurs in your Solar house of pleasure, leisure, romance and children bringing these areas of your life into sharp focus. You may be called upon to take a realistic view of a love affair that seems to be going nowhere…and think again. A choice awaits you there. Equally, a younger person may need your guidance and support while going through a difficult period.

FRIDAY, 24TH DECEMBER
Venus square Mars

Venus in a horoscope represents females (among many other things) while Mars represents males (among many other things). When these two planets are ninety degrees apart, this causes tension between the sexes. Therefore, today, you may be faced with a rabid 'woman's libber' or a true 'male chauvinist pig' of the old-fashioned kind. There is no point in arguing with such people, they are too full of their own opinions to listen. Where did the Christmas spirit go?

PISCES

SATURDAY, 25TH DECEMBER
Moon trine Pluto

If a present or a word of praise seems to be rather slow in coming your way, perhaps this would be a good time to tackle the subject. If others have made promises to you which have not been forthcoming, then remind them of their obligations. If you are fobbed off or given evasive answers, then ask for clarification, at least a good reason why you shouldn't be given what is your due. Apart from that, have a Merry Christmas!

SUNDAY, 26TH DECEMBER
Mercury sextile Mars

Though there may be problems at work, you can defeat all opposition with a little forethought. The shrewdness of Mercury unites with the strategic cunning of Mars to enable you to run rings around any opponent.

MONDAY, 27TH DECEMBER
Mercury trine Jupiter

Developments at work will be to your benefit now. Changes occurring further up the career ladder should hasten your progress. Apart from that, the cash front shows signs of improvement too!

TUESDAY, 28TH DECEMBER
Moon square Mercury

A surprise or two tend to be good for any relationship since they keep you on your toes. If you thought that you knew your other half inside out, then think again, because you'll be astonished by his or her actions and opinions now. It all serves to make life more interesting.

WEDNESDAY, 29TH DECEMBER
Moon square Sun

The insensitivity of some people you deal with in day-to-day life will dismay you greatly now. Sometimes it seems as if colleagues have no thought other than for their own advantage, and have no conception of any higher value. You, of course, are well aware of a more spiritual dimension to life but there's little you can do to change a materialistic outlook. At least you have a richer and more varied existence because of your beliefs.

THURSDAY, 30TH DECEMBER
Mars sextile Jupiter

Financially things are looking up, as inspiration strikes and you suddenly see a way

PISCES

to increase your cash potential. Your intuition mixed with clear thinking will show your economic life in a new light. Things are not as bad as you supposed for luck is on your side now. There's the likelihood of a profitable investment being made which will stand you in good stead for the future.

FRIDAY, 31ST DECEMBER
Venus into Sagittarius

If you're involved in any career in the arts, beautification, entertainment or public relations, then you're bound to do well in the coming year. Those who work for women bosses won't do badly either since a female influence in the workplace will aid your ambitions. Since Venus is the planet of charisma use diplomacy to solve professional problems. You can hardly fail to win with such a capacity for charm. Happy New Century!